Your Towns and Cities in the

❖

# Edinburgh
## in the Great War

Your Towns and Cities in the Great War

# Edinburgh
## in the Great War

**Derek Tait**

Pen & Sword
**MILITARY**

First published in Great Britain in 2016 by
PEN & SWORD MILITARY
an imprint of
Pen and Sword Books Ltd
47 Church Street
Barnsley
South Yorkshire S70 2AS

ISBN 978 1 47382 810 0

The right of Derek Tait, to be identified as the author

of th                                 the

A CII                               rary.

All rights                           ransmitted
in any                                uding
photoco                           etrieval
sy                                   g.

Typeset in Times New Roman

Pen & Sword Books Ltd incorporates the imprints of
Pen & Sword Archaeology, Atlas, Aviation, Battleground, Discovery,
Family History, History, Maritime, Military, Naval, Politics, Railways,
Select, Social History, Transport, True Crime, and Claymore Press,
Frontline Books, Leo Cooper, Praetorian Press, Remember When,
Seaforth Publishing and Wharncliffe.

For a complete list of Pen and Sword titles please contact
Pen and Sword Books Limited
47 Church Street, Barnsley, South Yorkshire, S70 2AS, England

E-mail: enquiries@pen-and-sword.co.uk
Website: **www.pen-and-sword.co.uk**

# Contents

*Chapter One*

# 1914: Eager for a Fight

Rising tensions in Europe and the assassination of Franz Ferdinand in Sarajevo on 28 June 1914 triggered the start of the First World War. Austria–Hungary delivered an ultimatum to the kingdom of Serbia and, on 28 July, declared war and invaded the country. The Central Powers, including Germany and Austria-Hungary, and the Allies, which included the British Empire, the French Republic and the Russian Empire, declared war on each other which led to the start of the First World War. Globally more than 70 million military personnel would be mobilised.

For the United Kingdom, what would become known as the Great War began on 4 August and triggered a wave of patriotism. Here Scotland led the way with 320,589 men voluntarily enlisting before conscription began in 1916. Scots were in the forefront of many of the costliest battles and campaigns with the outcome that, per head of population, it is estimated by the University of Edinburgh that Scotland lost more men than all the belligerent nations apart from Turkey and Serbia.

**On 4 August, newspapers posted announcements in their windows stating that Britain had declared war on Germany.**

On 5 August, the North British Railway Company had to close the Low Calton entrance to Waverley Station due to the large crowds of people who were visiting the station anxious to see the departure of trains carrying reservists and Territorials.

The *Edinburgh Evening News* reported the mobilisation of Territorials:

*Since the order went out to the Territorials to mobilise, the scenes at the various headquarters in the city have been of a most exciting description. In Edinburgh, the 4th and 5th Battalions (the Queen's Edinburgh) led the way and from 7 o'clock this morning, the men flocked in with full equipment to answer the call. So well did they reply that long before the members of other corps had put in an appearance at their respective drill halls, the baggage of the Queen's was being packed so that the battalions could leave at a moment's notice.*

1914: EAGER FOR A FIGHT    7

*In Leith, the 7th, which, by the way, claims to have had a larger proportion of its men than any other corps in Britain at the South African War, where it earned the name of 'The Fighting Fifth', mobilised early and before nine o'clock, its officers could say that it had turned out to a man. Before nine o'clock, the Royal Engineers, the only corps in Edinburgh which can keep up to its establishment strength, had turned out well, while many men of the Lowland Field Ambulance were also early on the scene. At the other headquarters, the men did not gather so quickly, as in some cases they did not need to be out before noon, while others were given to five o'clock to turn out.*

*Included among the latter were the Lothians and Border Yeomanry but the Field and Garrison Artillery started to mobilise in the forenoon and by a few minutes after ten o'clock, practically all the men had fallen in.*

*Needless to say, the mobilising created tremendous interest among the general public who hung round the drill halls all the morning. A curious fact about the crowds, however, was that they did not contain many young men but seemed to be composed of mainly old men and women folks.*

The Lord Provost, Malcolm Smith, visited the Drill Hall of the 7th Royal Scots in Dalmeny Street and addressed the men who were assembled nearby in a public playground. The men gave the Provost three cheers and he complimented them on their prompt response and their smart appearance.

Several football players were called up for service and these included George Sinclair, the Heart of Midlothian right-winger, and Neil Moreland, the centre-forward. Sinclair was an army reservist and was a member of the Royal Field Artillery. Moreland was a member of the Territorial Force.

The cost of some essential items, such as sugar, greatly rose in price when the declaration of war was announced. Previously sugar had sold for 15s 6s per cwt but was increased to 35s. Within a day, all shops were either sold out or in short supply as people rushed to buy in stocks. Flour and meal also disappeared from the shelves quickly.

*The Daily Record* of Wednesday, 5 August reported:

*The Glasgow Branch of the St Andrew's Ambulance Association have been asked by the Edinburgh section to forward any spare stretchers to North Queensferry. A considerable number of these were dispatched yesterday. It is conjectured that they will be utilised for a hospital base at Rosyth should Britain take an active part in the war.*

People of foreign descent were quickly rounded up and detained. Anyone with a German sounding accent soon came under suspicion of being a spy.

The railways were taken under government control under the Regulation of Forces Act of 1871. Local businesses were asked to supply motor vehicles for use by the army and businesses in and around Edinburgh were asked to supply horses.

A notice appeared in *The Daily Record* of 5 August stating:

*Special orders were issued last night empowering commanding officers to requisition horses and carriages, vessels and aircraft, and conferring authority on the officers to issue warrants on householders in any military districts for the billeting of troops.*

Horses fared badly at the front. Many were killed by artillery fire and were affected by skin conditions and poison gas. Hundreds of thousands of horses died during the conflict. Many horses were requisitioned from British civilians. However, Lord Kitchener stated that no horse under 15 hands should be confiscated. This was because many children showed a concern about the welfare of their ponies.

On 6 August, President Woodrow Wilson offered his services for mediation to all European powers involved in the war. He said: 'I should welcome an opportunity to act in the interest of European peace now or at any other time that might be thought more suitable, as the occasion might serve.'

On 7 August, the Prince of Wales started a National Relief Fund and appealed for people to contribute. The fund was set up to help the families of men serving with the forces and those suffering from 'industrial distress'.

*The Daily Record* of Thursday, 13 August reported:

*At the instigation of the Edinburgh Territorial Force Association, a City of Edinburgh Regiment is to be raised, to be handed over afterwards to the War Office. A central recruiting office will be opened in the Advocates' Library, Parliament House.*

The sum of £25 was donated by the Heart of Midlothian directors to the War Relief Fund opened by the Lord Provost of Edinburgh. Arrangements were also made for systematic collections at all home games of the club.

On Friday, 14 August, it was reported that the Prince of Wales's Fund had reached a total of approximately £35,000.

**On 19 August, President Wilson announced that America would remain neutral throughout the war.**

During August, the 3rd (Reserve) Battalion of the Royal Scots (Lothian Regiment) was formed in Edinburgh. They were a training unit and remained in the UK throughout the war.

The first shots by British troops on foreign soil took place on 21 August 1914. A military unit of the 4th Dragoon Guards, comprising of 120 men, were sent on a reconnoitring mission ahead of the British Expeditionary Force. Although members of the BEF had landed a week before, no contact with the enemy had taken place. As forces advanced into France and Belgium, they heard stories from civilians that large numbers of German troops were advancing towards the town of Mons in Belgium. Shortly after, the cavalrymen of the Dragoon Guards encountered the enemy and the first shots taken in Europe since the Battle of Waterloo became the first of millions to be fired over the next four years.

**Soldiers enjoying themselves in a boat on St Margaret's Loch during August 1914 while they await their instructions.**

**Recruitment at a football match during August 1914. Lord Roberts announced to the newly formed 10th Battalion of the City of London: 'I am proud to be the first to welcome you as brother-soldiers and to congratulate you on the splendid example you are setting your fellow countrymen.'**

**From 26–30 August Germany and Russia fought the Battle of Tannenberg resulting in the destruction of the Russian Second Army.**

On Tuesday, 1 September, the remains of German Naval Petty Officer Mayhofer were conveyed from Edinburgh Castle Hospital and interred with the accompaniment of full military honours. Petty Officer Mayhofer was one of the wounded men brought back to Leith on the previous Saturday after his ship, the *Mainz*, was sunk in the naval battle at Heligoland Bight. His condition was serious when he arrived and he died soon after being admitted to hospital.

His remains were borne on a gun carriage and interred at Echobank Cemetery. The coffin was covered with the German flag upon which was placed his naval cap. A firing party from the 5th (Queen's

Edinburgh) Battalion Royal Scots followed the remains. Also in the cortège were a number of German citizens living in the city. Included in the number were Professor Michael of Charlottenburg, who was temporarily in the city on account of being unable to get back to Germany, and Mrs Plathen, the wife of the ex-Austrian Consul, who placed flowers on the coffin which was carried to the grave by the Territorials.

The Lutheran burial service was conducted in German by the Reverend Hans Preplin. At its conclusion, the pastor said in English: 'Your nation and our nation are mourning for friends, but you as well as we are thankful that our friends have died as heroes. In this feeling we, even at this awful time of strife, are able to meet in prayer.'

He then repeated the Lord's Prayer in German and a number of the congregation joined in. Three volleys were fired over the grave and the Last Post was played.

The *Daily Record* noted:

> *The according of military honours at the burial of an alien enemy is unique in the military history of Edinburgh.*

**On 5 September, the First Battle of the Marne began. It also marked the commencement of trench warfare as both sides dug in preparing for combat.**

**Young men from Edinburgh practising volley-firing in preparation of being sent overseas into battle.**

**Mr George Hall, of 9 Murray Street, an old Scots Grey and a member of the National Reserve, was reported in September 1914 to have five sons and a grandson in the army. They were David Hall (Bugler in the 5th Royal Scots), A D Hall (Army Service Corps), Robert Hall (Royal Engineers), George Hall (National Reserves), John S. Hall (Royal Engineers) and George Hall, the grandson (Argyll and Sutherland Highlanders).**

*The Daily Record* of Tuesday, 8 September reported:

*Up to six o'clock yesterday evening 408 men had joined the service at Edinburgh and Leith from the opening of the recruitment offices in the morning. The flow of men is steady and continuous.*

All German and Austrian subjects in Edinburgh capable of bearing arms were taken into custody on Friday, 11 September. They were conveyed to Redford Barracks to join the large number of aliens already detained.

A meeting was held at the Council Chambers on Thursday, 17 September with the object of furthering the enrolment for the new City of Edinburgh Battalion. Lord Provost Inches presided and the members discussed the need for an appeal for recruits. The following evening, in the Usher Hall, men were given the chance to enlist. Four hundred names had already been submitted by men keen to join the battalion.

**The Edinburgh Territorials learning how to fire their rifles while training for action overseas.**

An advert appeared in the *Daily Record* of Saturday, 19 September. It read:

*Young men belonging to Edinburgh and the east of Scotland may enrol in the Edinburgh Battalion which is now being formed. All young men in the professional and commercial classes, university graduates, clerks, warehousemen, skilled artisans and athletes (between the ages of 19 and 35 inclusive), who are medically fit and whose height is 5ft 3 inches and upwards, with chest measurements of 34 inches at least, are invited to enrol their names now, and those of any friends who may wish to drill and train in the same battalion.*

*Enrol at once as it is intended to complete the battalion with all possible speed.*

Enrolment could be secured at 95 Princes Street, Edinburgh.

The *Manchester Evening News* of Thursday, 1 October reported:

*We are officially informed that the commanding officer of the Royal Scots, Edinburgh Battalion, is prepared to take a further 125 men of the Manchester Scottish, which will make in all 500 to be attached to this battalion.*

*All men of Scottish extraction who have already been attested, and others who have been enrolled, are asked to attend at the recruiting office, Albert Hall, Peter Street, Manchester, as soon as possible.*

*When the 500 has been completed it can be arranged to attach the surplus Scotchmen from Manchester to some of the Scotch battalions at present recruiting in Scotland.*

*A number of men left for Edinburgh this morning. They paraded in Piccadilly and marched down Market Street headed by Miss Marshall, of Oldham, a lady piper, to Victoria Station, where they entrained at noon for the North. A further batch of men will go to Edinburgh tomorrow.*

On Wednesday, 7 October, the *Daily Record* noted a famous recruit:

*Among the latest recruits to the Edinburgh Battalion of Lord Kitchener's new army is Roddy Walker, the former Heart of Midlothian back. He journeyed across from Fife on Monday and took the plunge. Two brothers and two chums joined with him.*

A report in the same newspaper noted that in a second distribution of funds collected at Tyneside that the Hearts' directors had sent £20 to the Prince of Wales's National Relief Fund, £20 to the Belgian Fund, £5 9s

4d to the Edinburgh Tramway Company's Cigarette Fund, and £5 5s to the Lord Provost of Edinburgh's Fund – a total of £50 14s 4d.

On Thursday, 8 October, it was reported that nearly 500 of the employees in Edinburgh Post Office were serving in the army or navy and, of that number, 415 had been drawn from the letter and parcel departments. The postal service had to be rearranged to take this into account resulting in three deliveries daily. The new system was said to be running smoothly and caused no inconvenience to the public.

Also on 8 October, it was announced that the Prince of Wales's Fund in Edinburgh amounted to £96,969 and the Red Cross Fund stood at £14,428.

In the second week of October, acting on instructions from headquarters, the Rothsay Burgh Police arrested five Germans capable of bearing arms and had them conveyed to Edinburgh.

An Indian Field Ambulance Training Corps was formed from Indian students in Edinburgh during October.

**On 19 October, the First Battle of Ypres began.**

**Edinburgh recruits receiving drill practice. Many hurried to join up and the men are shown here in October 1914 before receiving their uniforms.**

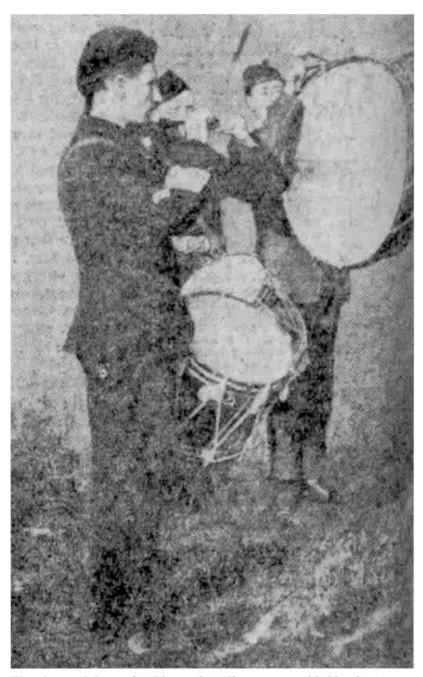

**The pipes and drums for this new battalion were provided by the
Edinburgh Merchant Company.**

The *Daily Record* of Friday, 30 October reported 'No Aliens at Edinburgh'. The story read:

*Edinburgh is now free from enemies. As the city is a prohibited area under the Aliens' Restriction Act, city officials yesterday saw that all aliens over 45 years of age carried out the portion of the act which requires them to remove to a free area. Notices to remove were issued to all aliens, comprising 88 Germans, many Austrians and one Hungarian. Glasgow and London were the places to which the majority of the aliens removed.*

On Tuesday, 3 November, it was reported that there were about 700 German and Austrian prisoners at Redford near Edinburgh. It was stated

that hopefully all would soon be moved to winter camps in England. In future, Edinburgh Castle was to be used for the reception of prisoners prior to them being transferred to detention camps.

On Wednesday, 4 November, it was announced that a consignment of tobacco and cigarettes to the value of £600 had been dispatched from Edinburgh to the front. The money had been collected by the employees of the Edinburgh and District Tramways Company. There were forty-six cases of tobacco and ninety-seven cases of cigarettes and a certain number of each was to be allocated to the different Scottish units. The total weight was nearly four tons, representing 26,000 1oz packets of tobacco and one million cigarettes. The order was made up by Messrs. McKinnell & Ross of Picardy Place, Edinburgh.

The *Daily Record* of Saturday, 7 November 1914 reported on 'Edinburgh's Own'. The article read:

*"A fine body of men well worthy of the name of the Edinburgh Battalion," was how Lord Provost Inches expressed his opinion of the city contingent of Lord Kitchener's New Army, after witnessing a march past of the Battalion in front of the City Chambers yesterday.*

*The Lord Provost and his colleagues in the magistracy and council graced the occasion by turning out in their robes of office. The Very Rev. Dr. Wallace Williamson, Mr A. Scott Dickson, K.C., M.P.*

**Sir Robert Cranston KCVO, who was the commanding officer of the Edinburgh Battalion of the Royal Scots.**

**Brigadier-General Kays passing along the ranks during inspection of the new battalion on 21 November.**

*and Mr G. W. Currie, M.P., were also among those present.*

*The Battalion is now 1068 strong and as it swung past to the strains of its fine pipe band, the physique and bearing of the men were very favourably commented on. Colonel Sir Robert Cranston was in command.*

On Saturday, 21 November, Edinburgh's Own gave an impressive turnout in the East Meadows where the corps was inspected by Brigadier General Kays, commander of the Lothian Brigade. Colonel Sir Robert Cranston was in command of the Edinburgh Battalion and there was a large crowd of spectators, keen to see the troop. The battalion subsequently formed up in front of Lord Provost Inches. Brigadier General Kays remarked upon their splendid appearance and said that they were a credit to all connected with them. As the men marched back

**The pipe band section of McCrae's Royal Scots battalion parading in Edinburgh during November 1914.**

to the Castle, accompanied by the music of the pipes, they created a highly favourable impression among the onlookers.

The *Daily Record* of Monday, 23 November of Sir George McCrae's new battalion:

> *Good progress continues to be made with the preliminary details in connection with the formation of a service battalion of the Royal Scots by Sir George McCrae. It is hoped that 250 men will be obtained from each of the four parliamentary divisions of Edinburgh. On Friday evening, a great recruiting evening will be held in the Usher Hall.*

Professional footballers were exempt from being called up, but on 25 November, eleven players from Heart of Midlothian enlisted for active service. Two more players joined the following day, making the number who enlisted sixteen, which included George Sinclair and Neil Moreland who were called up in August as Army Reservists.

In November, America sent a ship full of Christmas gifts for war orphans in Great Britain and other countries. American newspapers reported on 26 November that the 'Santa Claus Ship' was met with much joy when it arrived at Plymouth and Devonport had been festooned with decorations to welcome the Americans. Huge crowds gathered to welcome the *Jason* as warships directed it into the harbour. Lord Kitchener sent a message expressing the army's gratitude which was read at a banquet to the ship's officers.

The ship was loaded with 8,000 tons of gifts comprising of 5,000,000 separate articles which had been donated by American children and were destined for British, Belgian, French, German and Austrian children whose fathers were away fighting in the war.

The ship was officially welcomed by Earl Beauchamp, the president of the council, on behalf of the government. He was accompanied by Mr F.D. Acland, the Under-Secretary of Foreign Affairs, together with a large gathering of naval and military officers.

Among the greetings awaiting the ship was one from the Queen to the wife of the American Ambassador. In her letter, the Queen wrote: 'I am anxious to express through you my warm appreciation of this touching proof of generosity and sympathy and to ask you to be so kind as to convey my heartfelt thanks to all who have contributed towards these presents, which will, I am sure, be gladly welcomed by the children for whom they are intended and received with gratitude by their parents.'

The scheme was initiated by the *Chicago Herald* and a Mr O'Loughlin, who represented the journal, stated that 200 other newspapers throughout the United States had assisted in the project. As

**One of the first recruits being examined for Sir George McCrae's new battalion of the Royal Scots during November 1914.**

**Ladies of the Scottish Women's Hospital preparing to leave Edinburgh for France on 1 December 1914. Pictured are Nurse Conley, Miss Duncan, Miss Connell, Nurse Milne, Miss S.E.S. Mair, Miss Dorothy Littlejohn, Nurse Hogarth, Miss Swanston, Miss Maggie Gray and Nurse Maxwell.**

well as an enormous collection of toys, gifts also included shoes, boots, clothing, sweaters and stockings. So much was collected that 100,000 tons of presents had to be left behind.

While the *Jason* was at Plymouth, gifts were left for British and Belgian children before the ship carried on its journey to Marseilles to deliver presents to German children. It then carried on to Genoa to distribute gifts to further German and Austrian children. Gifts heading for Russia were loaded onto a different vessel.

The gifts were distributed all over Great Britain with Scotland getting its fair share. Female volunteers in Edinburgh happily sorted through them to give to children living in the city and surrounding districts.

It was announced on Saturday, 28 November that footballers and others interested in sport would be meeting in the Oddfellows' Hall, Edinburgh on the following Friday in connection with a Sportsmen's Company being formed in conjunction with the new Edinburgh Battalion.

Mr J.M. Hogge MP appealed to league players at Inverleith Park, Edinburgh to join up on Wednesday, 2 December. As a result, six members of the Edinburgh Nomads FC, one of the mid-week league clubs, enlisted together.

The *Daily Record* of Tuesday, 8 December carried a story under the From Newsboy to V.C.' It read:

*From the humble post of newsboy to the position of receiving the supreme award for military heroism – such is the record of Private George Wilson, of the Highland Light Infantry, who has just been awarded the Victoria Cross.*

*Only a few months ago, he was to be seen selling newspapers on the streets of his native city of Edinburgh. Then came the call to him as a Reservist and off he went after making the bantering remark to his sister that he would come home with the V.C. on his breast.*

*Private Wilson has been as good as his word; at all events, he has got the coveted cross to wear when he does come home.*

*Wilson was born and bred in the Lawnmarket of Edinburgh and some particulars of the daring deed that has brought him fame had arrived there ahead of the news of his honour. The circumstances are as follows:-*

*There was some severe fighting at the village of Verneuil on September 14th, the day on which Sir Archibald Gibson Craig made a charge and met his death at the head of sixteen men of the Highland Light Infantry.*

*Having ascertained that a German machine gun was stationed in a wood not far from the British lines, Wilson set out with a private of the 60th King's Rifles in the daring attempt to put it out of action.*

*Near to the enemy lines, Wilson had the agony of seeing his comrade shot down. Undeterred by this, however, he pressed on alone, shot down the officer and six men in charge of the gun and turned the quick-firer on the enemy.*

**The principals in Edinburgh's pantomimes. They were Miss Lily Morris, the principal boy in Jack and the Beanstalk at the King's; Miss Winnie Collins, the principal girl at the King's Theatre pantomime; and Miss Daisy Bray, the principal girl in Cinderella at the Theatre Royal.**

**The Edinburgh National Reserves on parade who numbered approximately fifty. Men were called upon to guard vulnerable points and lines of communication throughout the country.**

On Thursday, 17 December, one of the city's pantomimes, 'Jack and the Beanstalk', opened at the King's Theatre. Miss Lily Morris played the principal boy, Jack. It was her first time appearing in pantomime in Edinburgh although she was well-known in the city for appearing in the music halls. The principal girl, Princess Edwidge, was played by Miss Winnie Collins, who was also a popular entertainer in Edinburgh. The show was expected to be a huge success. Meanwhile, at the Theatre Royal, another pantomime was pulling in the crowds. 'Cinderella' starred Miss Edna Morgan as the principal boy and included special matinees for the Christmas and New Year holidays.

**Miss Edna Morgan, the principal boy in Edinburgh's Theatre Royal pantomime.**

**In some parts of the Western Front, on 24 December, an unofficial Christmas truce was observed.**

The *Daily Record* of Friday, 25 December reported on seasonal cheer in the city under the headline 'Khaki Christmas'. The article read:

*Edinburgh is not going to have the dull and dismal Christmas that was generally anticipated. There may be less disposition to festivity and merriment but in other respects the season of goodwill and*

The family of Private George Wilson waiting to greet him on his return to the city after being awarded the Victoria Cross. His brother, Corporal John Wilson, of the Royal Scots Fusiliers, invalided home from Ypres, can be seen in the doorway together with his sister, Mrs Devlin. Her husband, Driver Devlin, who was away fighting at the front, can be seen in the inset picture. Children from the tenement have also turned out to welcome the hero.

*good cheer promises to be as well observed as usual.*
*Frost held the city in its icy grip yesterday and made things congenial for the large crowds which moved about the streets.*

Recruits of the 4th (Queen's Edinburgh Rifles) Battalion of the Royal Scots marching through the city before they were issued with uniforms.

**Gifts from the *Jason* being packed into boxes ready for distribution to the children living in various districts of Edinburgh.**

*Khaki-clad figures mingled everywhere with shopping matrons and parcel-laden fathers. The large garrison of Territorials at present housed in and around the city was augmented by a considerable number of Regulars who had obtained a short furlough in order to be able to spend Christmas in the bosom of their families. More than one household was gladdened by the return of a weather-beaten warrior from the front.*

*Christmas Eve services drew out large congregations to a*

**Mounted troops of Sir George McCrae's new battalion parading through the streets of Edinburgh on Christmas Day.**

*number of the leading churches but, judging from the traffic in the principal streets, it would appear that a great many of the citizens spent the evening in making belated Christmas purchases. The gift-giving custom does not seem to be materially affected by the war.*

*The experience of the leading shopkeepers in the city is that the volume of the trade has been fairly well maintained but rather less money has been put into the presents and that articles of a useful nature have displaced the more luxurious gifts. This applies in some measure even to the toys for the children, in which connection it may be noted that the cheap 'Made in Germany' goods have for the most part proved a drag on the market.*

*The Post Office traffic has hardly come up to the usual dimensions. Christmas cards are not so numerous this year and the parcel delivery shows a drop to the extent of about 2,000. At the*

**McCrae's battalion pipe band proudly playing on the main thoroughfares of the city on Christmas Day. The inset photos show Captain Niven (left) and Major Clarke.**

*principal stations, however, the parcel as well as the passenger traffic has been well up to the usual proportions for this season of the year. The London trains were running three to four hours late yesterday in some cases in account of the abnormal amount of rolling stock on the lines.*

*Soldiers are, of course, being kept well in mind by the present-givers. During the past fortnight, large numbers of bulky parcels have been dispatched to 'Somewhere in France' full of articles that should do something to alleviate the hardships of life in the trenches. Nor are the soldiers at home being lost sight of. Sir George McCrae, for instance, will entertain his battalion to a Christmas dinner today after they have made a parade of the principal streets in their new uniform. From an old comrade-in-arms he has received the seasonable gift of a Christmas pudding for each of the men in the battalion.*

The *Daily Record* of Monday, 28 December carried a report of the recent Flag Day:

*A somewhat novel emblem was utilised in connection with a Flag Day in Edinburgh on Saturday on behalf of the scheme inaugurated by the Lord Provost's Committee for the supply of comforts to the Army and Navy. It took the form of a representation of the Blue Blanket, the flag of the ancient Incorporation of Edinburgh Trades, carried by them at Flodden.*

*A postcard which was also on sale gave the following statement with reference to the flag:- "This is Edinburgh's famous Blue Blanket and when it is unfurled, the citizens of Edinburgh are bound to come out under arms; they have fought beneath it well and often in times past.*

*When James III was imprisoned in the Castle, the Provost, Bailies and Councillors and citizens of Edinburgh with his brother, the Duke of Albany, stormed the Castle and rescued their King.*

*The King, in his Royal gratitude, conferred many favours on Edinburgh and the Queen and her women embroidered this banner for the craftsmen of the city."*

Towards the end of December, Kate Hume, aged 18, appeared in the Edinburgh High Court, before Lord Strathclyde. She was indicted for having concocted a letter with the intent of alarming and annoying the public, in particular, her father and her stepmother.

The allegation was that the accused forged a letter from her sister, Grace Hume, from Vilvorde near Brussels, to the effect that she had been murdered by German soldiers. The sister was alleged to be a nurse at the front and the letter told that she had died of her injuries. She was, in fact, in Huddersfield at the time.

Due to the sensational nature of the charges made by the accused, the case had aroused widespread interest. The court was packed when she took her seat in the dock. The prisoner who had been in custody for about three months was described as tall and good looking. She wore a fur toque and a serge cloak. She was said to be perfectly cool and self-possessed as she pleaded not guilty. She claimed at the time of the incident, her mind was unbalanced and she did not know what she was doing.

Evidence was heard from Andrew Hume, her father, who stated that there had been slight differences between the accused and her stepmother but these were only of a domestic nature. He first heard of the supposed murder of his daughter Grace in September in a letter which read: 'Dear Kate, – This is to say good-bye. Have not long to live. Hospital has been set on fire. Germans cruel. My breast taken away. Good-bye. Grace.'

There was also a letter from a nurse Mullard, who was supposed to be at the front, who had witnessed Grace's death and added: 'Grace requested me to tell you that her last thought was of her sweetheart and you were not to worry as she would be going to meet her Jock. One of the soldiers caught two German soldiers cutting off her left breast, her right one having already been cut off. Your sister was a heroine.'

**Sir George McCrae's battalion on a march-out through the city on Wednesday 30 December 1914.**

The witness said that he did not believe the story of his daughter's death and wrote to the War Office. In cross-examination, the witness stated that his son, John, had gone down with the *Titanic*. He was the leader of the ship's band which played 'Nearer My God To Thee'. The witness, speaking with some emotion, said that his son and the prisoner had been very close at which point the accused put her handkerchief to her eyes and silently wept.

The accused was later found guilty but was released on probation. The judge took into account her previous good character and the fact that she had already spent three months in custody.

# Chapter Two

# 1915 – Deepening Conflict

On 1 January, the Admiralty announced, through the Press Bureau, the capture of the German cruiser *Emden* by HMS *Sydney*. The report stated that the Germans had put up a poor fight.

A report on Wednesday, 6 January stated that recruitment had been much brisker in the opening days of January than it had been the some time previously. Approximately 130 men a day were being added to the strength by Captain Robertson and his staff.

A report in the *Daily Record* of Saturday, 16 January covered the enlistment campaign in the city:

> *Recruiting for the Regular Army in Edinburgh is proceeding very quietly and steadily. During the past few days, the average number of enlistments approximate between 50 and 60 and it falls to be noted that a good type of soldier is coming forward.*
>
> *In regard to the Reserve Territorial Battalions, the 4th Royal Scots is 42 over strength, while the 5th Battalion is 25 under strength, the 6th Battalion 158 under strength, the 7th Battalion 80 under strength and the 9th Battalion 180 under strength. The Reserve Company of the 15th Battalion Royal Scots (1st Edinburgh) is 20 over strength and the Reserve Company of the 16th Battalion Royal Scots (2nd Edinburgh) is also over the regulation number.*
>
> *Locally, the Territorial recruiting is at present much slower than for the Regular Army.*
>
> *During the past week or two, a substantial number of men have gone to the Royal Navy from the city, Leith and surrounding districts, particularly from places on the Firth of Forth.*

A long list of casualties, including both officers and men of the Expeditionary Force, was issued by the press bureau in January. It included the names of many Scottish men from the Gordon Highlanders, the Highland Light Infantry and the Royal Scots Fusiliers.

A farewell to the troops was reported in the *Daily Record* covering events on Thursday, 28 January:

> *Since the outbreak of the war, there have been many expressions of regret in Edinburgh that the gallant Camerons – whose valour had*

*added so glorious a chapter to Scotland's story – should have been practically smuggled away from the city without receiving any manifestation of the goodwill that went with them.*

*No risks are being taken with their successors in the occupation of the historic castle. A right hearty send-off was given today to the men of the 15th Royal Scots (1st City of Edinburgh Battalion), who departed, not for the scene of conflict on the continent but for their new training quarters in Ayrshire. Whatever the future may have in store for Colonel Urmston's men, they will at least have the satisfaction of knowing that the people of Edinburgh take a keen interest in their welfare.*

*This is as it should be, for, although the battalion contains probably as many Manchester Scots as Edinburgh men, the fact cannot be overlooked that it represents the first contribution of the Scottish capital to Kitchener's Army. Nor can the citizens fail to observe how the raw material of three months ago has gradually developed into a first-rate fighting unit.*

*As the battalion swung down the Castlehill and along Princes Street one heard on every side expressions of admiration at the fine bearing and physique of the men. They have improved immensely in appearance since the khaki clothing and equipment was served out in place of the former uniform.*

*Three special trains have been requisitioned to convey the battalion west, the men marched from the Castle to Princes Street Station in three detachments of about 250 each, leaving a reinforcement company to occupy the depot at Castlehill School under the charge of Colonel Sir Robert Cranston.*

*On the way the music of the pipes in the 'Seventy-ninth's Farewell to Gibraltar' mingled with the cheers of the onlookers who lined the streets, more especially in the vicinity of the station. The first and last contingents were headed by the battalion pipe band and the middle lot had a like service done them by the pipers of the 4th Royal Scots (Queen's Edinburgh), who also stayed to play, "Happy we've been a thegither" as the train steamed out of the station.*

*The good spirits of the men were testified by many a hearty cheer and many an attempt to break into song. The crowds around the precinct of the station responded with equal heartiness and the battalion must have carried off the most happy memories of its Edinburgh leave-taking.*

*If the enthusiasm was less robust than would probably have been the case had the men been on the point of leaving to play their part in the theatre of war, there was none of that depression of spirits which can never be far distant from a farewell taken when the dangers of battle are imminent.*

*The first train left at 10.20 for Troon and the two others departed at intervals of forty minutes with Prestwick as their destination. Colonel Urmston having gone ahead with the advance party earlier in the week, the entraining arrangements were supervised by Major Rose, assisted by Colonel Cranston.*

*Lord Provost Inches and some of his colleagues put in an appearance to take leave of the battalion and among others on the platform was Dr. Patrick Mackay, chaplain to H.M. Forces in Scotland.*

*After entraining, each of the men was supplied with a meat pie to fortify him against the journey. There were also a number of friends who came forward with supplies of reading matter. Thus provided, it was a happy and contented body of men that steamed out of the station, their own lusty cheers mingling with those of the crowd that had assembled to wish them Godspeed.*

In the House of Lords, in reply to a question by Lord Moncrieff, Lord Lucas stated that the drab kilts that were being issued to Scottish

**Adjutant J.B. Bruce (left) with Colonel Urmston of the 15th (1st City of Edinburgh) Battalion of the Royal Scots watching their men depart Edinburgh for their new training quarters in Ayrshire on 29 January 1915. They were given a hearty send off.**

**A group of German sailors who were rescued from the *Blücher* by HMS *Arethusa*. They were fitted out at Edinburgh Castle with thick, warm clothing. They are seen here being marched to their quarters under armed guard.**

regiments was only a temporary measure because a sufficient number of tartan kilts couldn't be supplied in time.

On the afternoon of Thursday, 18 February, thousands of people in

**The funeral in Edinburgh during February 1915 of Major Alexander Scott of the Royal Garrison Artillery. The photo shows a detachment of men from the Royal Garrison Artillery with reversed arms.**

**Colonel A.S. Blair, Commanding Officer, and Captain R.M. Dudgeon, Adjutant, of Edinburgh's 'Dandy Ninth'. Earl Rosebery stated: We are confident they will distinguish themselves and bear the name of old Scotland with glory.'**

**A big procession of pack mules, to be used for military purposes, was paraded through Edinburgh on 16 February 1915.**

Edinburgh turned out to pay their respects to Carl Erdnann who had died after being recovered from the sea after the sinking of the German war cruiser *Blücher*. The vessel had been destroyed in the North Sea engagement by Admiral Beatty's squadron on Sunday, 24 January. His remains were interred in the Echobank Cemetery in the city.

Captain Erdnann was brought to the city suffering from shock and the effects of exposure. He was expected to recover but died in the Edinburgh Castle Military Hospital on Monday, 15 February.

The funeral was timed to leave the Castle at 3pm but before the time arrived, a crowd of thousands had gathered in the vicinity of the Lawnmarket and the Castle Hill. The streets were packed and the general sentiment was one of respect. In order to get a clear view of the funeral, a large number of people found their way to the Castle Esplanade but the military police moved them on so that the cortege could pass.

A number of recruits of the 15th Service Battalion of the Royal Scots were drilled under the command of Sir Robert Cranston. They drew to attention as the funeral procession emerged from below the Castle Gateway and gave a salute as the funeral party passed slowly.

The coffin was borne on a gun carriage by members of the 11th

**Impressive crowds turned out for the funeral of Carl Erdnann on Thursday 18 February 1915. The German cruiser, *Blücher*, had been sunk by Admiral Beatty's squadron during the Battle of Dogger Bank.**

Battery London RFA Brigade which was in the charge of Sergeant McCallester. The coffin was covered with the German flag with the Double Eagle accompanied by three floral tributes from the crew of the *Blücher.*

In front of the gun carriage, the detachment of the Royal Scots, who were to serve as the firing party, marched slowly carrying their rifles reversed. They were preceded by two officers carrying their swords in an attitude of mourning. Immediately behind the gun carriage, Herr Planer of the German Lutheran Church was the chief mourner and behind him followed two naval officers, Lieutenant Commander Hurt and Lieutenant Hodge. They were followed by Captain Rutherford who was in charge of the Royal Scots and other members of the detachment.

The pipe band played 'The Land of the Leal' as the procession made its way from the Castle down the Esplanade and the Castle Hill. Throughout the long route to the cemetery there were dense crowds. Five thousand people waited at the cemetery gates at the Newington entrance. The solid oak coffin was lowered into the grave and a volley of shots were fired by men of the Royal Scots. After several people gave speeches, 'Lochaber No More' was played by a lone piper before 'The Last Post' was sounded by members of the Royal Scots buglers.

**On 19 February, the Dardanelles Campaign began.**

Towards the end of February, Corporal Robert Kelman, of the 1st Dragoon Guards and a native of Edinburgh, was mentioned in despatches by Sir John French. While out sniping with the Dragoons, a bullet grazed his head. He was returned home and took a position as a drill instructor at York.

It was announced on Monday, 1 March that carters' wages would be increased by 3 shillings in the city. This made the weekly wage 25 shillings and 26 shillings for single horse drivers and 20 shillings for pair horse drivers.

**The band of the Newfoundland troops who were on garrison duty in Edinburgh during February 1915. They received a cordial welcome from the Lord Provost when they arrived to take up their quarters at the castle.**

**The death occurred at Edinburgh Castle on 20 February of another German sailor, a further addition to the list of victims on the ill-fated warship *Blücher*. The funeral on 23 February was attended with less ceremony than on previous occasions but the cortege was headed by a military band.**

On Wednesday, 3 March, a soldier appeared before Sheriff Maconochie at Edinburgh and pleaded guilty to four acts of shopbreaking. The articles stolen included six pairs of opera glasses, nine pairs of eyeglasses, five boxes of artificial eyes, two watches and a chain, a waterproof coat and 5s 6d in money. It was stated that the accused, who was 27 years old, was home on furlough after serving in France and was found in one of the shops with part of the stolen property in his possession.

The Prosecutor suggested that as he had not appeared in court before, he should be given the benefit of the Probation of Offenders Act. He was put on probation for six months with a view to him being taken back into the army.

It was reported on Friday, 5 March that operations at the Dardanelles were having an effect on the price of flour. The Edinburgh and Leith

Flour Millers' Association reduced the cost by 1s per sack. The prices were: whites 52s per sack; extra 51s; supers, 50s.

On Thursday, 11 March, the *Daily Record* carried a story under the headline 'Echo of the Blücher'. It read:

*A detachment of 25 of the crew of the German cruiser* Blücher *were transferred from Edinburgh Castle to Stobs Camp yesterday evening.They were under a guard drawn from the 1st Newfoundland Regiment and the route to the Waverley Station was made in the most unostentatious manner. The sailors, who were clad in civilian clothes, were those who have got the better of their wounds and the effects of their immersion in the water when the* Blücher *was sunk. They looked quite happy and unconcerned and a number of them were smoking pipes and cigarettes. The most of them carried bundles.*

On the morning of Friday, 12 March, a Red Cross train arrived at Edinburgh carrying over one hundred disabled soldiers. Apart from a few cases of frostbite, most of the men were suffering from wounds. Fifty of the soldiers were taken to Craigleith, thirty to Dalmeny and thirty to the Deaconness Cottage Hospital.

On Saturday, 13 March, it was announced that a nurse who had left Edinburgh for Serbia at the end of 1914 had succumbed to fever. Nurse Margaret Neill Fraser had been a prominent figure in the golfing world and she played regularly in the Open and Scottish Ladies' Championships. Her companion worker, Nurse Louisa Jordan from Glasgow, also succumbed to the fever which was ravaging the country.

On Thursday, 18 March, trains from Edinburgh to London were greatly delayed because of a heavy snowstorm. The 10.17 train arrived three and a half hours late at Newcastle and deep snow lay all the way damaging cables and signals. On Monday, 5 April, it was reported in the *Edinburgh Evening News* that Mr and Mrs William Millar of 107 Trinity Road, Edinburgh, had received intimation that their son, Private John Trotter Millar, of the 2nd Battalion Middlesex Regiment, had been killed in action at Neuve Chapelle on 14 March.

On Wednesday, 7 April, Isabella O'Brian appeared in Edinburgh Sheriff Summary Court. She pleaded guilty to having neglected and ill-treated her two daughters, aged five and nine years, and of putting herself persistently into a state of intoxication making it impossible for her to care for her children.

The prosecutor stated that the accused was spending the money she got from the War Office on drink. She was drawing 17s 6d a week of separation allowance and spent it all on alcohol. Her rent was paid by her husband's employers, he was at the time on active service with the Highland Light Infantry.

Sheriff Orr said it was deplorable that this kind of conduct should go on after all that had been done for the accused. He stated that he must put her out of temptation's way and sentenced her to two months' imprisonment.

A female sympathiser shouted to her in court saying 'Cheer up, hen!'

On Saturday, 10 April, the *Daily Record* announced that Commander Henry Peel Ritchie had been awarded the Victoria Cross. He was the first member of the Royal Navy to receive the award in the First World War. The son of a prominent Edinburgh doctor, he was born in the city in 1876. He was awarded the VC for a meritorious deed performed on HMS *Goliath*. The citation read:

> 'For most conspicuous bravery on the 28th November 1914 when in command of the searching and demolition operations at Dar-es-Salaam, East Africa. Though severely wounded several times his fortitude and resolution enabled him to continue to do his duty inspiring all by his example until at his eighth wound he became unconscious. The interval between his first and last severe wound was between twenty and twenty five minutes.'

For six weeks, he had been recovering from his wounds at his home in Glencairn Crescent, Edinburgh. Previously, he had been confined to hospital at Zanzibar. When the *Daily Record* interviewed him on Friday, 9 April, he had been restored to good health and had been passed for shore service. The newspaper noted:

> *He is a keen follower of manly sport and is known thoughout the Navy as one of its most expert boxers. He was an amateur lightweight champion of the Army and Navy in 1900 and in the following year he went to the final of the same event.*

On Thursday, 15 April, the 17th (Rosebery's Bantams) Battalion of the Royal Scots took part in their first public parade which included marching past the Earl of Rosebery. The battalion was under the command of Colonel Cheales.

The *Daily Record* of Saturday, 17 April published a notice about the city's street lighting:

> *The Lord Provost, with the approval of the military authorities, intimates that until further notice, the public gas lamps in the city will not be lit and the electric lamps will be extinguished at 12*

*o'clock. It is further requested that the citizens will take care that all windows of houses and buildings where lights are used shall be obscured by use of blinds or shutters.*

**At the Second Battle of Ypres, beginning on 22 April, the Germans used poison gas for the first time.**
**On 25 April, the Gallipoli Campaign began.**

At 2.30pm on the afternoon of Monday, 3 May, the daughter of a serving soldier on active service was killed in Dundee Street, Edinburgh. Martha Pryer, aged two, was being wheeled along the pavement in a go-kart when it hit a kerbstone and the girl fell out on to the road where she was hit by a passing horse. She was killed instantaneously.

**On Friday 7 May, the ocean liner RMS *Lusitania* was sunk by a German U-boat leading to the deaths of 1,198 of which 128 were Americans. The sinking enraged the Americans and hastened their entry into the war.**

On Saturday, 8 May, the various units of the Edinburgh Boys' Brigade were inspected in the city by the Marquis of Linthithgow. There was a large turnout for the event.

On Sunday, 9 May, Jens Mathisen, captain of the Norwegian steamer *Scotland*, anchored his ship at the May Island contrary to the Defence of the Realm Act. He was fined £20.

On Wednesday, 12 May, it was announced that Lieutenant Colonel James Clark, the 56-year-old commander of the 9th Battalion of the Argyll and Sutherland Highlanders, had been killed at Ypres. He was a prominent citizen in Edinburgh and well respected in the city.

During the second week of May, a resolution in favour of compulsory service was unanimously adopted by the Edinburgh Territorial Force Association. The matter came before them after a request from the Northumberland Territorial Association asking for their support.

On Friday, 14 May, a warning was given by Edinburgh Sheriff Court to landladies with alien lodgers. Three landladies and two lodgers, a Japanese doctor and a Brazilian student, appeared in connection with failing to furnish particulars necessitated by the Aliens' Restriction Order. Each of the accused was dismissed with an admonition by Sheriff Orr. He stated that the police had considerable difficulty regarding the registration of aliens living in apartments and the cases dealt with were

**Funeral procession for victims of the Gretna rail disaster, 1915.**

intended to draw to the attention of keepers of apartments the need to register aliens residing there.

On Tuesday, 18 May, news reached Edinburgh that Private Archibald Wilson, of the 2nd Cameron Highlanders, had been killed in action during the previous month. He was 20 years old and had joined the army three years previously. He attained such proficiency with a rifle that he was regarded as a crack shot in his regiment. His home was at Buccleuch Street, Edinburgh.

On 22 May, over 200 soldiers from the 7th Royal Scots were killed when they were involved in a multi-train collision at the Quintinshill signal box near Gretna Green.

**Charred remains of a carriage involved in the Quintinshill crash.**

The first crash took place when a southbound train carrying soldiers on its way to Liverpool hit a stationary local train. The wreckage of that crash was then hit by a northbound express sleeper train from London Euston heading towards Glasgow. Gas from the train's lighting system ignited, led to a fire which soon engulfed five trains. It remains Britain's worst railway accident.

The *Western Daily Press* of Monday, 24 May reported:

*Under existing conditions the spirit of Whitsuntide would have this year been chastened, but the gloom has been accentuated by the railway disaster which occurred near Quintinshill, a small wayside station near Gretna Green Junction. The disaster is one of the most appalling of its kind in the history of British railways. Not two, but three, trains were in collision, and the result was that about one hundred and fifty persons lost their lives, and over two hundred suffered more or less grievous injury. The disaster happened shortly after dawn, and the scene has been represented as almost indescribable. One of the trains wrecked had on board some five hundred officers and men of the regiment of the Royal Scots. Many of these soldiers had seen service at the front in Flanders and in France, and one of them is reported to have said that nothing he had seen in the trenches was nearly as bad as the havoc and suffering caused by the smashing of the troop train. The cause of the disaster is yet to be definitely ascertained; but the layman is able to see that one principal contributory cause was the shunting of a local train on a main track over which one or more expresses were almost due to travel.*

This report, so soon after the accident, understated the extent of the catastrophe. In fact almost half the soldiers on the troop train were killed; 212 of them Territorials from the 1/7th (Leith) Battalion of the Royal Scots on their way to Gallipoli, along with civilians including children. More than 240 more were injured.

Over one hundred of the soldiers were buried in a mass grave at Edinburgh's Rosebank Cemetery after a mile-long procession through the city streets lined with thousands of troops.

During a boxing match on the evening of Monday, 24 May, Tancy Lee knocked out Private Young Dando in five rounds at Edinburgh. The bout took place in the Synod Hall with an audience of 2,000. The contest was set for fifteen rounds but Lee was the stronger boxer and had his opponent repeatedly down for the count. In the third round, Dando was four times on the floor.

On Tuesday, 1 June, the *Daily Record* featured a story about the number of policeman in the city joining the army:

*There will be no shortage of recruits of a particular fine type if the example of the Edinburgh Police Force is followed throughout Scotland.*

*Yesterday afternoon in Parliament Square, an interesting little ceremony took place, when Chief-Constable Ross bade farewell and God speed to nearly 100 of the members of the police force who have been released from duty to enlist in the forces of the Crown.*

*In the course of a short address, the Chief Constable said he was glad the men had made such a response to the call. They had been called upon to perform a very serious duty and he was sure they would behave as soldiers as they had as policemen.*

*The Corporation appreciated very highly what they had done and on Saturday, he had received a letter from HM Secretary of*

**Edinburgh teams took part at the military sports and fete at Peebles on 19 June. The event included the bethroning of the Beltane Queen. Miss Jeannie Fleming played the queen and she can be seen being conducted to her throne.**

A procession of small girls in white dresses, tartan sashes and glengarrys paraded along Princes Street on 19 June bearing banners which encouraged men to enlist in the 4th Royal Scots.

Sir Joseph Fayrer inspected the 12th Edinburgh Company of the Boys' Brigade at Victoria Hospital on 19 June. The hospital was being used as a convalescent home for wounded soldiers. Major Robertson VC, who was in charge of the Army Recruiting Headquarters in Edinburgh can be seen behind Sir Joseph.

*State for Scotland expressing satisfaction at their action. He was satisfied that when the time came when they faced the enemy they would give a good account of themselves. The Chief Constable then shook hands with each of the men and wished each of them God speed.*

*A short address was also delivered by Colonel Sir George McCrae who remarked that it did not matter what unit a man joined as long as he served his country at the present time. It was the duty, he emphasised, of every able-bodied man to go forward.*

*The majority of those who were present have passed the medical examination for enlistment in the Seaforth Highlanders and this makes a total of nearly 200 all told who have, since the outbreak of the war, joined the fighting forces of the Crown from the ranks of the police force.*

*The policemen were in grand fettle and they were a specially fine looking body of men, who will not only show the kilt to its best advantage, but who may be relied upon to give a capital account of themselves in action.'*

The *Daily Record* of Thursday, 10 June reported on recruitment in the city:

*Edinburgh continues to do well in the matter of recruiting and a good type of soldier is coming forward. A goodly number of men are being enrolled daily, both at the offices at Cockburn Street and at 71 Princes Street. The Rosebery Bantam Battalion of the Royal Scots is to be increased by another company of 250 men, bringing the strength up to 1600. The recruiting offices are at 2 Castle Street, Edinburgh, where respective recruits will be cordially welcomed.*

It was reported towards the end of June that Private John Pyper, who returned to the front after recovering from a wound, was shortly afterwards killed. He was a member of the 1st Gordon Highlanders and had seen service with the battalion in both India and South Africa. His widow resided at Crosscauseway, Edinburgh. He is commemorated on the Menin Gate Memorial, Ypres.

On the afternoon of Saturday, 3 July, between sixty and seventy skilled tradesmen were registered at the City Chambers, Edinburgh, to join the ranks of munition workers. This brought the total up to over 350. At a mass meeting of Edinburgh and Leith Electrical Trade Unions, it was agreed to favour the munitions registration scheme.

On 12 July, the *Edinburgh Evening News* carried the story of a recent recruiting drive:

*A recruiting effort was organised on Saturday night in West Princes Street Gardens, Edinburgh, by the Rosebery Royal Scots Recruiting Committee. Music was discoursed by the band of the 3rd Royal Scots, which attracted a large crowd, although this was considerably thinned as the speaking was to begin by a sharp shower of rain. Baillie Rose presided and explained that the battalion it was immediately sought to assist was the 7th Royal Scots now fighting at the Dardanelles. He said that those who joined the colours did not regret the step but felt the satisfaction that they had done their duty. What the people had to do now was to enlist, to work and to lend.*

*Provost Malcolm Smith, Leith, gave as an indication of the right spirit which should animate the people, the willingness of a man in San Francisco, who was 58 years old and who wrote him that he would come all the way back to Leith if he could do anything to help. There should be no need of talking now, for everyone understood the situation. In the 7th Royal Scots, which was the*

**Girl telegraph messengers were the latest innovation in Edinburgh in August 1915. At the time of the photo, the girls hadn't been issued with a uniform but a badge was worn to indicate their official position.**

*Leith Battalion, recruits from Edinburgh would be welcomed.*
*Many Leith men were in Edinburgh battalions. Edinburgh and*
*Leith were amalgamated as far as that was concerned and they*
*were prepared to co-operate in all good work.*

On Saturday, 17 July, Edinburgh held a Badge Day to raise money for
British soldiers interned in Germany. On the eve of Badge Day, the
skipper of the fishing boat *Isa* asked his crew if they would agree to give
the proceeds of the night's fishing to the fund. They all agreed. They
had a successful night and handed over a cheque for £3 10s. Altogether,
the Badge Day raised a total of £1,342 3s 7d.

On the afternoon of Sunday, 18 July, to celebrate the second
anniversary of the Northern Men's Federation for Women's Suffrage, a
demonstration directed towards the subject of women and the war was
held in the East Meadows, Edinburgh. Delightful weather prevailed and
large crowds gathered around each of the three platforms. There were
Edinburgh, Glasgow and Berwick-on-Tweed platforms. Mrs Arncliffe
Sennett spoke saying that the motto of the afternoon was, 'In our unity
lies our strength.' She urged electors to enlist themselves under the
banner of the federation. Councillor Graham stated that the war was
giving them a new conception of sacrifice and that women should have
the equality of citizenship. He instanced the success of the women
tramway conductors in Edinburgh for whom there had been secured the

**Convalescent soldiers in Edinburgh helping with gardening and
haymaking. The man shown is supported by crutches as he helps to move
the hay.**

**Wounded soldiers housed at St Leonard's in Edinburgh helping out with gardening work.**

same terms and the same conditions in regard to the rate of pay per hour as men.

Councillor Barrie said that while women currently fight for their emancipation and rights, it was the men who had the vote and were able to make the situation of women more equal.

The councillor paid tribute to the women in St Leonard's Ward in which there were already twenty widows in consequence of the war. One woman, with four young children, to whom he offered sympathy on the loss of her husband, bravely replied: 'He heard the call. He went. He has done his duty and I don't grudge him going.' The councillor stated that that was the spirit of the women of the country today and hoped that they would, at some future time, receive equal rights and pay.

More news on recruiting appeared in the *Daily Record* of Tuesday 27 July:

> *The fourth and last of the recruiting weeks set apart in Edinburgh for the benefit of the local Territorial battalions was entered upon yesterday when a crusade commenced on behalf of the 9th Royal Scots, familiarly known as 'The Dandy Ninth'. The severe fighting in Flanders has made inroads on the strength of the battalion and the recruiters are out to get 163 men to bring the third line up to establishment.*

The *Daily Record* of Saturday, 7 August carried a story about the 'dauntless Argylls'. It read:

> *Private Daniel Kelly, 5th Argylls, who is in the Royal Infirmary, Edinburgh, describing his experiences at Achi Baba writes:- "It was a terrible charge and the Argylls covered themselves with glory. I cannot praise my officer, Captain Agnew, too well. When I last saw him, he had his revolver in one hand and his helmet in the other, waving us to come on.*
>
> *I think that I'm the luckiest chap in the whole battalion. We were in the enemy's third trench when I was tumbled over. I thought that it was a large shrapnel bullet that struck me but judge of my surprise when the doctor told me it was a small one and that it had gone through my eye and right into the back of my head, where it finally stuck in a bone. I have lost my eye but I'm lucky to be alive."*

On Friday, 20 August, an Edinburgh chaplain, the Reverend David Paterson, who had been serving at the front, appealed for magazines and books for the troops which were much enjoyed by the wounded in hospitals in France.

The *Daily Record* of Monday, 23 August reported a case of enemy betrayal:

> *German treachery of a particularly despicable kind was responsible for the death of Lieutenant J.A.E. Alexander, Highland Light Infantry.*
>
> *In a letter to his mother, who resides at No 1 Howe Street, Edinburgh, the commanding officer of the battalion says the lieutenant stopped his men from firing at one of the enemy who*

**Scots Greys carrying the coffin of Private James Christie in Edinburgh during September 1915.**

**Pipers playing a lament at the graveside of Private James Christie.**

*had crept up on the British trenches and he went out with three men to take this man prisoner.*

*When being brought in, the German pulled a pistol out and shot the lieutenant in the back, having previously called for mercy by calling 'Kamerad, kamerad.*

The *Edinburgh Evening News* of Wednesday, 25 August carried an advert stating that lice were a soldier's biggest enemy in the trenches. The advert recommended Somerville's 'Asiatic Body Cord' which promised to exterminate all body lice and prevent them from lodging on a person or their underclothing. It was available by mail for 1s from Somerville Chemist, 2 South Clerk Street, Edinburgh. Postage was 1d inland or 2d to the trenches.

**Private Robson VC aiding recruitment in Edinburgh gardens while encouraging men to enlist in the Royal Scots during September 1915.**

On Saturday, 28 August, a military band played in the Scottish Zoological Park in Edinburgh between 7pm and 9pm in the evening. In the interval, there was a short address from Major W. Robertson VC of the Gordon Highlanders, and Sergeant John Ripley VC of the Gordon Highlanders concerning recruiting in the city.

A flag day was held on Saturday, 4 September to help raise funds for disabled soldiers and sailors who had been discharged from the army or navy.

**On 5 September, Tsar Nicholas II took over control of Russia's armies.**

A Red Cross train was taken to Edinburgh where it was displayed at Princes Street Station until the second week in September. It was described as a 'hospital on wheels' and was used to treat wounded soldiers returning from the front. A large number of visitors came to look at the train and the admission charge went towards the Red Cross fund. The Dowager Duchess of Roxburghe performed the opening ceremony. Sir M. Mitchell Thomson recalled that over 40,000 people had visited the train when it had previously been displayed at Glasgow.

The *Daily Record* of Wednesday, 8 September carried a story under the headline 'An Edinburgh Hero'. It read:

*Word has been sent to Edinburgh of the death from wounds in the Greek hospital at Alexandria of Lance Sergeant T. Alison, 5th Royal Scots, who resided with his father at 9 Plewlands Terrace. He was a splendid type of young man, being 23 years of age and 6ft. 4in. in height.*

*In the course of a letter received by his father, it is learned that Lance Sergt. Alison met a hero's death. Some of the wounded of the 5th Battalion were lying beyond the shelter of a trench which he had gained. Hearing their moans and cries for help, he went to their rescue and, with several others, carried six wounded men to safety. Four of them were now recovering. In a charge that took place shortly afterwards, Sergeant Alison was killed.*

On Wednesday, 15 September, the trial began in Edinburgh of two signalmen and a fireman who were charged with causing the train crash at Quintinshill near Gretna in May. The hundreds who had been killed and injured due to their breach of duty included 212 men from the 7th (Leith) Battalion of the Royal Scots; Henry Ford, engineer; Samuel Dyer, railway saloon attendant; Lieutenant James Crawford Bonnar, Lieutenant John Jackson and Captain Robert Finley of the Argyll and Sutherland Highlanders; Lieutenant Commander Charles Head of the Royal Navy; Francis Scott, train driver; James Hannah, fireman, and a mother and her young son.

All the accused entered pleas of not guilty. Thirty-two witnesses were to be heard for the prosecution. Eventually the two signalmen primarily responsible, George Tinsley and George Meakin, were sentenced to three years and eighteen months' penal servitude respectively. The fireman, George Hutchinson, was acquitted.

On Friday, 17 September, a triple murder and suicide took place in

**Several members of the 7th Royal Scots attended the court during the trial of the railwaymen.**

**Women coal-carters at work in the West End of Edinburgh during October. The women were described by the *Daily Record* as 'simply splendid'. Here they can be seen carrying coal into various houses in the city.**

Edinburgh. A medical student named William Juta, from Pretoria, had been attending medical classes at the university. Six years earlier, Juta had married Muriel McGregor of Carnoustie, the daughter of William McGregor, a tea planter in India. They had one son together. On the evening of 17 September, Juta shot his wife, child and mother-in-law. He later took his own life in the South African Union at 14 Buccleuch Place, of which he was a member. He left a letter which read: 'Good-bye, my fellow countrymen; I wish to die among my friends.'

An article in the *Daily Record* of Saturday, 2 October reported on a parade in Edinburgh:

*Imposing as have been some of the recruiting parades already held in Edinburgh, that which takes place in the capital today bids fair to eclipse them all.*

*Two brigades of artillery and many battalions of infantry are to take part, following a route from the King's Park that will take them to Princes Street via Abbeymount, Easter Road, Dalmeny Street,*

**Gallant Gordons home on leave from the trenches. The men were photographed as they passed through Waverley Station in Edinburgh on their way home to the North during September 1915.**

*Leith Walk, York Place and St Andrew Street. The start-off is timed for 2.30. Recruiting meetings are to be held at different points along the route and among the speakers will be Mr C.E. Price, MP, and Mr G.W. Currie, MP.*

On the morning of Sunday, 3 October, several soldiers, all from Edinburgh, were run down by a train while on the Forth Bridge. Two were killed, including the officer in command, Captain Miller, and a private. Nine other men were injured.

Traffic on the Sunday was limited to one line but there had been a misunderstanding over which line was being used. The *Lincolnshire Echo* reported:

**Brave Seaforths on furlough, home from Flanders. They were also photographed at Waverley Station during September.**

**Two men are seen with a recruiting poster outside the Royal Naval Division recruiting headquarters in Edinburgh. The poster was designed by Chief Petty Officer Flynn and showed a turkey. The recruit in the photo was a science student in the city.**

*The men were marching two abreast and were in the last cantilever when a train came on their side of the line and before anything could be realised, the captain, who was marching behind, was caught by the engine and flung in front of the train. The force with which he was thrown forward brought some of the men down and, in a twinkling, ten men were mixed up in the wheels of the train. The thirty men were all carrying their equipment and, with their rifles and baggage, they were simply crammed into the insufficient space between the train and the bridge edge. The train was brought to a standstill with little delay and the officials ran to the help of the soldiers.*

*Captain Miller was found cut to pieces and Gunner Sinclair was also dead. The others injured were Corporals Petrie, King*

**Wounded soldiers taking a stroll in Edinburgh accompanied by a nurse in November 1915.**

*and Robb; Trumpeter Pennaird, Gunners Stewart, Adams, Henderson and McLaren.*

*Aid was telephoned for to the Craigleith Military Hospital near Edinburgh and, with all speed, motor ambulances and medical men arrived at the bridge. The injured men were conveyed to Craigleith. Late at night, six of the injured were reported to be in a serious state.*

On Monday, 11 October, Mr W.M. Ramsay JP, presided in the Church of Scotland Young Men's Guild Tent at the Portobello Chocolate Works at an entertainment given to soldiers quartered in the area. Mr Ramsay announced that the marquee was soon to be replaced with a more permanent building made of wood which would include kitchen accommodation, a reading room and a post office. A concert was given for the wounded soldiers and several local artistes gave their services.

The *Daily Record* of Saturday, 5 November carried the story of an Edinburgh bride's sad fate:

*The East Sussex coroner held an inquest yesterday in the parlour of the coastguard's house at Birling Gap, on Isabel Mackenzie Sampson, wife of Lieutenant St John Sampson, Army Service Corps, who met her death by falling in a motor car from the cliff near Belle Taute lighthouse.*

*Lieutenant Sampson states that he and the deceased were married in Edinburgh on Wednesday, October 27. He was not sure of her age but thought she was 31. Mr Kirkwood, the deceased's brother, questioned on the point, said that his sister was 35 or 36.*

*Lieutenant Sampson, continuing, said they stayed in London for five days and on Monday evening last, arrived at Eastbourne. On the following day, they motored to Birling Gap and, with the intention of visiting the lighthouse, left the car pointing towards the cliff. They found the lighthouse locked and his wife returned to the car.*

*The witness saw her sitting in the car but when looking up after passing behind some furze bushes, his wife and the car were gone. The witness was in a very bad state of mind for a few minutes. He took it that the car was over the cliff because the whole place was bare. He did not go and look over the cliff as he did not think he was physically capable of doing so.*

*The witness went to a cottage and told the people that there had been an awful accident. Lieutenant Sampson added that the car was of American make and had an electrical starting apparatus operated by a small lever on the dashboard. It was an extremely simple arrangement. The lever was moved by the driver's hand.*

*Mrs Sampson could not drive a car. The only thing she knew how to use was the self-starter. The witness thought that in a childish way, she was proud of doing it, in fact, she did it that morning outside their hotel while witness was there.*

*Asked by the Coroner if he was aware of anything that might possibly make his wife desire to take her own life, Lieutenant Sampson replied – 'On the contrary, I don't think my poor wife was ever so happy in her life. I am as certain of that as I am that I am sitting here at this moment. She was absolutely happy.'*

*Mr William Brown Kirkwood, solicitor, of Blackford Road, Edinburgh, brother of the deceased, deposed that on Tuesday, he received from the deceased a letter in which she said she was perfectly happy. She was exceptionally timid but she might have touched the starting lever of the car to show her husband that she understood it.*

*Thomas Akehurst, a roadman, gave evidence confirming that of Lieutenant Sampson. The witness saw the lady in the car by herself. He thought he heard an aeroplane and looked up. When he looked again, the car and the lady were gone.*

Among the flag sellers for the Lifeboat appeal in Edinburgh on 6 November were Miss Mabel Munro and Miss Fernan, two well-known actresses who had appeared in the musical comedy *The Pearl Girl.*

*The jury returned a verdict of accidental death and expressed profound sympathy with Lieutenant Sampson.'*

On Saturday 6, November, a reception was given to members of the overseas forces currently in the city. The event was held at the City Chambers during the evening. The men were formally welcomed by the Lord Provost and Brigadier General Maclachlan who declared that finer fellows one could not wish to meet than those who had come from overseas. Corporal Collins from New Zealand returned thanks. The function was enjoyed by all.

An advert appeared in the *Daily Record* of Tuesday, 9 November appealing for 250 men to join McCrae's Battalion (16th Service Battalion of the Royal Scots). Those interested were asked to enlist at the Recruiting Office at Palace Hotel, 1 Castle Street, Edinburgh.

On Saturday, 20 November, several passengers were slightly injured

Convalescing Australian soldiers are pictured purchasing Lifeboat Saturday flags in Edinburgh from Miss May Moore Duprez, the popular music-hall artiste.

**The entire mail staff of the Caledonian Station Hotel in Edinburgh enlisted under the Derby Scheme in December 1915. Some of the men can be seen pictured with the chief chef of the hotel. He was a loyal Frenchman who left to join his country's army at the beginning of the war.**

when the surburban train they were travelling on collided with an engine at Waverley Station. The accident happened at 9 o'clock in the morning and the train was filled with passengers coming into the city to work.

On Tuesday, 30 November, St Andrew's Day was observed in Edinburgh by a memorial in St Giles' Cathedral for Scottish soldiers who had fallen in the war. There was a brief service in the Chapel of the Thistle attended by the Knights and Officers of the Order. Afterwards, the Knights passed into the church to join the public service which was attended by the corporation and other representative bodies.

It was announced in the newspaper on Wednesday, 8 December that Second Lieutenant James McKenzie, of the 10th Seaforth Highlanders,

had been killed by a sniper in France. He was a graduate of Edinburgh University and had won the Van Dunlop scholarship of £100 for three years before proceeding to Cambridge University.

A gypsy troupe who were engaged to appear at the Edinburgh Carnival at Christmas were prohibited from travelling to the city on Wednesday, 15 December. They were stopped within the restricted **A Red Cross sale began in Edinburgh on 2 December. All the articles were donated by various members of the public and local businesses. The photo shows a Shetland pony which was to be sold for the cause.**

area of Midlothian and told that they couldn't proceed any further without passports. Mr Townsley Cyril of the Gypsy Club in Regent Street, London visited them at Pathead where they were temporarily encamped with their animals while waiting for advice what to do next.

An article appeared in the *Daily Record* of Tuesday, 21 December under the headline 'No New Year Drinks'. It read:

*The magistrates of Edinburgh decided yesterday to recommend that licence holders should not open their premises on New Year's Day. The Liquor Board of Control had issued a recommendation that licensed premises should only be open between the hours of four and nine.*

The *Southern Reporter* of Thursday, 23 December reported on the Christmas pantomime in the city:

Wounded soldiers from all the military hospitals in Edinburgh attended a concert in the Usher Hall on 2 December. The men were conveyed to and from the hall in donated vehicles.

*The pantomime 'Little Boy Blue' is now in full swing at the Theatre Royal, Edinburgh. On this occasion, an important departure is made from the long-established custom, for the pantomime is playing twice each night. The explanation is that the change is made to keep 'moving with the times'. The Brothers Egbert are the principal comedians, Miss Pearl Gray is the principal boy and Miss Haidee de Rance the principal girl. Special holiday matinees have been arranged.*

Meanwhile, 'Dick Whittington' was being performed at the King's Theatre. It began its run on Thursday, 16 December and starred Miss Lily Morris as Dick Whittington and Miss Elise Frasetti as Fairy Sunbeam. Also appearing in the production, as the cat, was Eddy Foy.

The *Daily Record* of Saturday 25 December carried the news of Christmas time in the city:

**Miss Violet Egbert, the Fairy Queen in Little Boy Blue, the Christmas pantomime at the Theatre Royal.**

*The weather in Edinburgh yesterday was not at all in keeping with the traditional Christmas. The day was raw, with a good deal of haze, and walking was*

A large number of troops in the city had to return to the trenches before Christmas Day. Here is one of the soldiers seen posting his Christmas cards to friends before returning to battle.

Scottish troops returning home from the trenches for Christmas complete with toys for their children.

Three Scottish nurses from the National Union of Women's Suffrage Society's Hospitals arrived back in Edinburgh from Serbia during December. They were pictured at Waverley Station and were Miss Gordon, Miss Bell and Miss Neish.

**The arrival of Christmas puddings at the front brought much excitement from the troops. They can be seen receiving puddings and other gifts from home.**

*very unpleasant owing to the damp and greasy state of the streets. Christmas shopping was in full swing and during the afternoon the Princes Street shops reaped a big harvest. Everybody practically was carrying parcels and it was manifest that the children were not forgotten. From the crowds on the main thoroughfares, and from the busy conditions noticeable in the different shops, it was quite apparent that money was not scarce. The usual watchnight services were held in the Roman Catholic and Episcopal Churches.*

*Traffic at the railway station and post office was unusually heavy and the number of letters and parcels disposed of were quite as numerous as last year. A number of local soldiers are home on a few days' furlough from the Front.*

Towards the end of December, it was announced that armlets would be

**A soldier home from the trenches for Christmas welcomed by his family,
Some of the troops were lucky to get a few days' leave over the holiday
period.**

issued to all men who had been rejected from the army and navy on
medical grounds. Those who were certified medically unfit were only to
be registered while those who were rejected on account of eyesight or a
slight physical defect were to be attested and passed on to the Army
Reserve. They would then be liable to be called up at any time for
medical examination and for service in any occupation in which a soldier
may seem considered suitable by the military authorities.

*Chapter Three*

# 1916 – The Realization

As the new year rolled in, the *Daily Record* reported on the events on 1 January:

*A violent south-westerly gale, accompanied by heavy rain squalls, was the experience of Edinburgh on New Year's Day. A large number of people came into the city from the country districts and their position was a sorry one.*

*The most of the shops were closed for the day and the recommendation by the magistrates as to the closing of licensed premises was very generally observed. All the public offices were closed and business throughout the city was at a standstill. At the railway stations, a heavy incoming traffic was disposed of, a large number of soldiers on leave making their arrival. At the different Presbyterian churches, services were held.*

*Edinburgh police report having had the quietist New Year for many years. The number of arrests over forty-eight hours was under 100.*

On the afternoon of Friday, 14 January, a reception was held in the city for the members of the hospital units that had recently returned from Serbia. The event was held under the auspices of the Scottish Women's Hospital for Foreign Service. Altogether, about 300 men and women received a hearty welcome. Twenty members took part in the retreat across the mountains to Montenegro and Albania.

A graphic account of the hospital work in Serbia was given by Dr Beatrice McGregor who said that her party were inclined to be a little downhearted now and then but stated that all the sisters were very brave. She mentioned that there were six nurses in her unit who had all nursed typhus cases all during the previous winter and she was very proud of them for their pluck and endurance under difficult conditions.

The Very Reverend Dr Wallace Williamson voiced his thanks and stated: 'The heart of Scotland, and indeed the heart of the Empire, are very grateful to the Scottish Women's Hospitals for the very noble part they took in the sacred ministry of healing, which alone relieved the gloom and did much to eradicate the horrors of the war.'

**Members of Edinburgh University Officers' Training Corps who were inspected by Lord Provost Sir Robert K. Inches in the High School yard during January 1916. They can be seen in the photo receiving instructions on how to fire a gun.**

Mrs Lawrie voiced the thanks of the executive for the wonderful support they had had for their scheme. In the fifteen months it had been running, they had received over £80,000 and seven units had been equipped and sent out.

On the call of Miss Mair, a hearty round of applause was given for Dr Elsie Inglis and Dr Alice Hutchison who were still in Serbia.

On Saturday 29 January, Lord Rosebery inspected the Edinburgh Volunteer Training Corps at Saughton Park.

On Wednesday, 2 February, an advert appeared in the *Daily Record*

appealing for marines aged 17 to 38 as well as navy men to act as seamen, stokers, cooks' mates, coopers, engine-room artificers, fitters, armourers, ship wrights and electrical artificers. Boys were also required aged 15½ to 17 for long service or the duration of the war. Applicants were required to apply at 8 Johnston Terrace, Edinburgh.

**Major Mackenzie, who was in charge of the Officers' Training Corps, can be seen with two members of his staff while Lord Provost Inches inspects his troops.**

**Pantomime artistes visiting wounded solders in Bangour Military Hospital on 3 February. The actors all came from the Theatre Royal in Edinburgh where they were appearing in 'The Babes in the Wood.' They made the journey to the hospital by car where they entertained the delighted troops.**

On Thursday, 3 February, a fine of £40 was imposed at Edinburgh on James Rosie, the master of the British vessel *Ravenna*, for having taken his vessel into the Firth of Forth when there was not sufficient daylight to reach Inchkeith before official night. He explained that due to engine trouble, he was unable to reach the examination ship in time.

A case of a missing soldier writing home was reported in the *Daily Record* of Friday, 4 February:

*Since he was posted as missing after the battle of Mons, nothing had been heard of Private Robert Panton, 2nd Royal Scots, until yesterday, when his mother, who resides at 35 Dumbiedykes Road, Edinburgh, received the glad tidings that he is safe, though a prisoner in the hands of the Germans. He has only now been able to get through a letter from his quarters in the Kriegsgefangenenlager, Merseburg, Germany.*

Also on Friday, 4 February, it was mentioned at the annual meeting of the Edinburgh and District Tramways Company, in reply to a question from a shareholder, that the women conductors were doing a better job than the men. It was also stated that no tramway company in Great Britain had so small leakage in the collection of fares as the Edinburgh company.

**Three jolly little Jack Tars who took part in the entertainment in Waverley Market during February. The event was opened by Lord Strathclyde.**

On Thursday, 10 February, an art exhibition, in aid of the fund for soldiers and sailors blinded in the war, was opened at Shandwick Place, Edinburgh by the Countess of Elgin.

Sir Frederick Milner, presiding, explained that the money collected went towards helping blinded men at St Dunstan's Hospital in London. He said that the ex-servicemen there were provided for and trained in various occupations suitable for their condition. He also said that they were extremely happy and contented.

After a graceful speech, Lady Elgin declared the exhibition open. There was a large attendance.

**On 21 February, the Battle of Verdun commenced. It proved to be one of the longest and bloodiest of the war.**

The *Daily Record* of Monday, 21 February carried the story of a hare hunt in Edinburgh:

*The unusual spectacle of a hare hunt in the streets of Edinburgh was witnessed on Saturday shortly after mid-day.*

*A surprise was given to several dozen*

**Mr Mark Lester carrying Miss Nellie Taylor over the step into Craigleith Hospital where the company of 'The Miller's Daughter' entertained the wounded troops.**

*people in the vicinity of the post office, when puss came trotting in the direction of Waterloo Place from the North Bridge. Keeping up a steady pace, the hare easily outdistanced her pursuers, and one or two of the more venturesome, who tried to make her run into their arms, got somewhat nasty falls by tripping themselves in their over anxiety to make a capture. The animal dodged quite a formidable array of assailants and made a gallant dash towards the Calton Hill.*

*When last seen, puss was going at about the rate of about 90 miles an hour towards the sanctuary of the Regent Terrace Gardens, with several persons in keen pursuit, and to the accompaniment of encouraging cries from a number of spectators with sporting instincts who stood aside to give the hare a good chance of escaping.*

*A number of the would-be captors exchanged words of comfort at their loss and no doubt ruefully recalled the commandment of the old recipe of hare soup, 'First catch your hare.'*

On 29 February, the British auxiliary *Alcantara* sank the disguised German light cruiser, *Greif*, in a battle in the North Sea. The A*lcantara* was also destroyed by German torpedoes with the loss of many lives. Several German sailors were rescued and taken to Edinburgh Castle where they were later imprisoned.

**In March, compulsory enlistment for men between the ages of 18 and 41 was introduced for single men and childless widowers. However, essential war workers, clergymen, the physically unfit and approved conscientious objectors were exempt. The upper age was later raised to 51.**

A story appeared in the *Daily Record* of Tuesday, 7 March under the headline 'A Fearless Soldier'. It read:

*Official intimation has been received in Edinburgh that the Commander-in-Chief, by permission of the King, has awarded the Military Cross to the late Lieutenant Robert M. Murray, RGA.*

*Lieutenant Murray died on February 25 from injuries received in the field. The Brigadier General, in intimating the award, of the Military Cross wrote: "He was absolutely fearless and will be a serious loss to me and to his battalion."*

*Lieutenant Murray was 22 years of age and was the youngest son of the late Mr A Murray, GSO, secretary of the local government board for Scotland.*

**Ladies of Edinburgh packaging fruit ready to be sent to Scottish soldiers at the front. The ladies were associated with the Edinburgh Dried Fruit Society. Miss Macfarlane, the daughter of Councillor Macfarlane, organised the proceedings and was the honorary secretary.**

On Monday 27 March, a complaint was made at a meeting of the Edinburgh and Leith Corporations Gas Commissioners regarding the shortage of coal. Over the previous few months, almost 20,000 tons of coal had been removed from the Commissioners' stores to make up for deficient deliveries. It was stated that action would have to be taken through the Board of Trade to guarantee sufficient supplies throughout the winter season.

Also on 27 March, the *Daily Record* carried a story about German prisoners being taken to Edinburgh Castle after the recent conflict in the North Sea:

> *On Wednesday, 1st inst., rumours were rife in Edinburgh that there had been an engagement in the North Sea and colour was lent to these by the arrival at Leith of a number of German sailors. These were disembarked at Leith Docks from which the public were rigidly excluded and the contingent were placed in three large motor buses and taken to Edinburgh Castle for confinement. There were also two or three Red Cross motor ambulances which conveyed the wounded.*
>
> *One of the Germans was dead when the party landed and his funeral took place at Seafield Cemetery, Leith. The coffin, over*

*which was placed the German flag, was conveyed from the Castle to the cemetery on a gun carriage drawn by horses. In front of the carriage was a party of sixteen men from a Scottish regiment, while in the rear were three German sailors followed by two members of the military police. In a closed cab were two German naval officers and the assistant Provost Marshal. The funeral during its long course to the cemetery was respectively saluted by members of the public to the evidently expressed surprise of the Germans, who had anticipated that it would evoke quite different feelings from the populace.*

*During a subsequent week, the funerals of two German sailor prisoners have taken place from Edinburgh Castle to Seafield Cemetery. The coffins, wrapped in the Imperial German flag, with the black eagle, were conveyed to the cemetery on gun carriages attended by German officers and men who are also prisoners at Edinburgh Castle.*

On Monday, 3 April, it was reported that there had been fewer cases of drunkenness during the first quarter of the year. Crime, on the whole, had shown a general decrease apart from that of juveniles. During the previous three months, 1,880 people came before the courts compared to 2,840 in the same period during 1915 and 3,967 during the same three months of 1914.

The offences showing the biggest decrease related to drink. However, the number of women arrested for insobriety increased in 1915 and this mainly included offences by soldiers' wives.

The *Daily Record* of Tuesday, 25 April carried a report about spring visitors to the city on Easter Monday:

*There was a large influx of holidaymakers to Edinburgh yesterday where delightful weather prevailed, except for a strong wind, which made the parading of the streets a trifle uncomfortable. Besides doing the rounds of the customary sights of the city, some of the visitors enjoyed the spectacle of a cable car breaking down – a sight that has lost all its novelty for Edinburgh people but one that apparently had a good deal of interest for the holidaymakers.*

William Hughes, the prime minister of Australia, visited Edinburgh on Wednesday 26 April. While there, he was given the freedom of the city and presented with an honorary degree from the university. The ceremony of conferring the freedom of the city took place in the Usher Hall. Lord Provost, Sir Robert Inches, presided over the meeting in front of a large crowd.

Mr Hughes paid tribute to Scotland for what she had done in the war and said that the end was not yet in sight. After a long, well-applauded speech, he stated: 'If we devoted all our energies to the great end then we and our Allies will march to triumphant victory.'

This was followed by loud and prolonged cheers. The function was concluded with a luncheon in the city chambers.

On Friday, 28 April, the *Daily Record* carried a story under the headline 'Curious Incident at the Police Court':

> *An unusual incident happened in Edinburgh police court yesterday morning. John King Maxton, artist, residing at 16 Scone Gardens, walked into the dock and addressing Bailie Archbold, who was on the bench at the time, said: "Your Honour, I desire to be arrested."*
>
> *Mr Weston, Clerk of Court, stated: "Go down to the Charge Office." Mr Maxton replied: "Arrest me as a deserter under the Military Service Act. I have come to state my reasons." Mr Weston asked Mr Maxton to stand aside, as he had no status before the court.*
>
> *Mr Maxton afterwards explained to the police officials the reason of his conduct. His total exemption card, as a conscientious objector, from the Recruiting Tribunal, had been withdrawn by the military authorities and, as a result of the recent police court cases, he was entitled to a respite of two months before joining the Army. He said that he did not want the concession. He further*

**The Russian Council of the Empire and Duma visited the United Kingdom during May to see first hand what Britain was doing towards the success of the war. They arrived in Edinburgh by special train from Glasgow on 16 May. In the photo can be seen Mr Ian Malcolm MP and Mr John Buchan together with some of the visitors.**

**Large numbers of convalescing soldiers took advantage of the warm weather in the city during May 1916. The men here can be seen strolling through Princes Street Gardens.**

*declared that he was now out of work. No one would employ him and he was walking about the streets unable to get work.*

On Tuesday, 16 May, a special delegation, containing members of the Russian Council of the Empire and the Duma, arrived by train in the morning in Edinburgh after travelling from Glasgow. They were welcomed by Lord Provost Inches. Afterwards, the party proceeded to the Caledonian Station Hotel whilst acknowledging the greetings of a small crowd which had gathered to see them.

The guests arrived in London, on invitation of the government, on Saturday, 6 May so they could see the great part that Britain was playing in the war. While in the country, they visited munitions factories and military camps, attended civic meetings, and enjoyed entertainment in London and Glasgow as well as Edinburgh.

On Thursday, 18 May, the body of Private W. Bell, of the Gordon Highlanders, was found on the beach at Balgownie Links, Aberdeen. He had been missing from camp since 21 April. He was a native of Edinburgh and after serving time in France, he was invalided home. His remains were moved to the mortuary at Lodge Walk.

On Friday, 19 May, the 11.30am East Coast express from King's Cross to Edinburgh met with an accident at Scremerston, three miles south of Berwick. The tender and eight coaches left the tracks and ploughed along for about 400 yards causing considerable damage to the platform. No one was injured in the accident and the passengers and mail were transferred to another train and taken to Edinburgh where they arrived two hours behind time.

At the conclusion of the public business of Edinburgh town council on Wednesday, 24 May, Lord Provost Inches said that he wanted to read out a letter which he had recently received. It was from Vancouver in Washington and read:

*Dear Lord Provost and town councillors of the city of Edinburgh, I have to confess that I did steal an apple from a stand of some description in the Cowgate as far back as about forty years ago and I send you a dollar as payment, to be used in whatever way you think best and I want you to forgive me for it. David Masterton.*

Councillor Macfarlane suggested that the dollar bill might be given over to the care of the corporation museum but the Lord Provost gave the money to the care of the City Chamberlain.

The *Sunday Mirror* of Sunday, 28 May carried a story of three girls who had gone missing in Edinburgh:

*The Midlothian police are endeavouring to solve the mysterious disappearance of two Edinburgh girls.*

*Lillias Davies Gray, aged fifteen, was last seen at a band performance in Edinburgh last Tuesday, while another girl, named Margaret McNeil, has been missing for ten days.*

*After going for a walk last Sunday with her soldier sweetheart, Grace Parker, a young tobacconist's assistant, living at Mabledene Road, Dalston, was not seen again until Friday, when her body was recovered from the River Lea, near Lea Bridge. She is described as a girl of a happy, light-hearted disposition, immensely proud of her soldier lover. He was stationed at York and came to London to see his relatives.*

**On 31 May, the Battle of Jutland began, a major naval battle crucial to winning the war.**

On 5 June, Lord Kitchener was killed while onboard HMS *Hampshire*. The ship hit a mine which had been laid by a German U-boat. In total, 643 of the 655 crew, including Kitchener, drowned or died of exposure.

The *Daily Record* of Thursday, 8 June published the contents of a telegram sent by the king to Lord Provost Inches regarding the death of Lord Kitchener. It read:

> *I much appreciate the expressions of sympathy which you have conveyed to me from the citizens of Edinburgh in the grievous calamity which has befallen the Empire by the death of Lord Kitchener.*

On Tuesday, 13 June, a memorial service was held for Lord Kitchener at St Giles Cathedral, Edinburgh. It was attended by naval and military representatives as well as delegates from civic, academic, official and professional bodies. The building was crowded and most of the men there were members of the army or navy. The Reverend Dr Wallace Williamson, Dean of the Order of the Thistle, was the preacher and the lessons were read by Professor Sir Ludvic Grant of Edinburgh University.

Officers wearing sombre service dress dominated the congregation. Admiral Sir David Beatty was among those present.

On Thursday, 15 June, a general meeting of the Edinburgh Merchant Company took place which called upon the government to take steps to ensure that all alien enemies, naturalised or not, were interned for the duration of the war.

Mr James Mackenzie proposed the motion and said that the heads of communities in Edinburgh and Glasgow were told that they could do nothing. He said that this was because there were too many Germans in high places and, to save these men, the community must live in jeopardy. After deliberation, the resolution was carried by 33 votes to 12.

The *Edinburgh Evening News* of Thursday, 22 June reported on the recruitment drive in the city:

> *As the recruitment campaign for voluntary enlistment draws to a close, the open-air meetings held by Major Robertson VC, are attracting bigger and most interested crowds. At the Tollcross meeting last night, the Major and the other speakers addressed a very responsive audience and the band of the 3rd Boys' Brigade played selections. Among those who took part in the proceedings was a private of the Royal Scots Bantam Battalion, who was wounded in France by a fragment of shell and who has lost his left hand.*

*The little men had a great reception in France on their arrival and as they proceeded to the war zone. In marching and in their behaviour in the trenches, the Bantams have already proved their grit. The Germans appear to have sensed somehow the arrival of the Bantams in the trenches opposite, for they began bawling challenges at them at night and mockingly calling 'Cock-a-doodle do.' The little men did not disclose their identity but boldly called on the enemy to attack if they dared. Not a German ventured to leave his trench against them. The appreciation of the Bantams is shown by the fact that they were sent forward to relieve in the trenches one of the most distinguished of our regiments, many of who are giants compared with the Bantams.*

*The meeting tonight to be addressed by Major Robertson VC, and others, will be held in Nicolson Square at 7.30. The band of the Royal Blind Asylum will play selections.*

**On 1 July, the Battle of the Somme began. The British Expeditionary Force suffered almost 60,000 casualties on the first day, with 19,240 men killed, making it the bloodiest day in the history of the British Army.**

On Saturday, 1 July, the *Bury Free Press* carried a story under the headline 'Mistress Killed by Servant Girl'. It read:

*In the High Court in Edinburgh on Tuesday, a servant girl of 15 was sentenced to ten years' detention on a charge of having, on March 23rd, in a house in Peebles, assaulted her mistress with an axe and killed her. On account of the girl's youth, the Crown made the charge of one of culpable homicide to which the girl pleaded guilty.*

*Counsel on her behalf emphasised the extraordinary lack of balance by the girl and explained how, after the commission of the crime, she dressed herself in her mistress' furs and took the train to Glasgow.*

*The Solicitor-General characterised it as a deplorable case. The girl had a most unfortunate career and was really a person of incorrigible criminality and a danger to society.*

As the Battle of the Somme raged in Europe, relatives in Edinburgh dreaded a knock on the door, as they had throughout the war, of the telegram boy bringing news of their loved ones' death. Newspapers carried the news of all wounded and killed soldiers.

At the beginning of July, Galashiels Angling Association sent 64lbs of trout to wounded soldiers in Edinburgh Infirmary.

On Monday, 3 July, it was announced that coopers in Edinburgh had made an application to the master brewers for a minimum wage of 42s 6d a week.

On Tuesday, 11 July, the Edinburgh Territorial Force Association's Sports Committee met in the TFA rooms to discuss the forthcoming sports event which was to be held at Tynecastle, Edinburgh on 29 July in aid of the Blinded and Disabled Soldiers' Fund.

Ten Scottish league clubs agreed to send teams to take part in the five-a-side football competition.

On Monday, 17 July, it was announced that Newington House was to be used as a training hostel for Scottish soldiers and sailors who had lost their sight in the war. With the view to making them independent, reading of Braille was to be taught as well as typewriting. No charge was to be made for residence or training and the men who attended were to be given full support in finding new work when the course was over.

The *Daily Record* of Monday, 17 July reported that there was currently an epidemic of juvenile crime in Edinburgh. In just one day, twenty-eight boys and girls had appeared before the Children's Police Court.

**A sports day for wounded soldiers was held at Grange Sports Ground, Edinburgh on 22 July. Mrs Gardiner presented the prizes to the successful competitors.**

**J.H. Motion, of the Eglinton Harriers, shown beating George Malcolm, of the Edinburgh Southern Harriers, in the one mile open handicap at a sports day held at Ardrossan during July.**

During the third week of July, a flag day was held in Edinburgh for the purpose of supplementing the income of old-age pensioners in the district.

On Tuesday, 1 August, the King's Own Scottish Borderers held their Athletic Sports Day at Duddingston Camp, Edinburgh. The band of the KOSB was present. Entry to the event was free to everyone.

The *Daily Record* of Friday, 18 August carried a story concerning problems with an upcoming football match:

> *Two factors are likely to operate against the complete success of the Heart of Midlothian. Unless the services of Nellies and Mercer are fully available – a point on which there seems some ground for doubt – the club can hardly hope to attain to its usual high standard at half-back.*
>
> *Again, a good deal depends upon the extent to which the soldier-players are able to get off from military duties. Sergeant Miller and Private J Wilson are quartered a good many miles south of Edinburgh and Willie Wilson is just as far away to the north.*
>
> *In the circumstances, it may be supposed that only now and again will all three be seen in the team. A long journey like that to Greenock puts Mr McCartney "up against it" right off and not until tomorrow will he be able to make certain of his team. He has some good young talent at hand but against the Morton "old firm" it is of course desirable that seasoned players should be turned out as far as possible.*

On the evening of Thursday, 24 August, Viscount French spoke at Edinburgh and declared that the Territorials had practically saved the country. He assured new volunteers that they would be valued greatly. The distinguished field marshal was in the city to inspect the National Reserve of the City and the 1st Edinburgh Battalion of Volunteers. The ceremony took place on the Meadows and a large crowd of spectators witnessed the event. Despite the dull weather, many thousands of people were present.

The men on parade numbered 1,432 consisting of 526 members of the National Reserve and 906 Volunteers. Having taken the salute, the field marshal went around the ranks and spoke to many of the men gathered there.

After the ceremony, Viscount French addressed the leaders of the Volunteer movement and stated that it gave him great pleasure to visit Scotland and witness the fine military spirit which he saw displayed everywhere.

Towards the end of August, Mary Forsgood was sent to prison for four months at the Edinburgh Sheriff Court for ill-treating and neglecting her three children. She was the wife of a soldier and received an allowance of 23s a week.

After the sentence, her husband made an appeal for leniency. He stated that he had been at the front for eight months and had been home wounded and was soon to return. He said that it wasn't much of a holiday to come back to this sort of thing. The Sheriff pointed out that the children would be well looked after.

In the *Dundee Evening Telegraph* of Friday, 1 September, a story appeared under the headline 'German Gun For Edinburgh'. It read:

*One of the Royal Scots battalions which has figured with credit in the great offensive which commenced on 1st July suffered previous to that date what is described by one of the officers as "much annoyance" from a 12-inch canister thrower operating from the German lines opposite their trenches. When the British line advanced this large-calibre weapon fell into their hands. Intimation has now been made that the captured trophy is to be handed over to the battalion in question to commemorate their share in the action. The gun, which is complete with base block and elevating gear, is to be forwarded to the Lord Provost of Edinburgh and will remain in his custody.*

At the beginning of September, the Glasgow, Edinburgh and Dundee offices of the No-Conscription Fellowship were raided by the police who seized all copies of a pamphlet which gave a verbatim report of the recent Mansion House proceedings against the Honourable Bertrand Russell. The police also took samples of other pamphlets and leaflets found on the premises. The Edinburgh offices of the Independent Labour Party were also raided.

The *Aberdeen Journal* of Saturday, 2 September carried the story of a Scottish piper's bravery:

*A remarkable exploit by an Edinburgh piper in the great offensive has been specially signalised by the French war authorities. The piper is Sergeant (Acting Pipe-Major) D. Anderson who was formerly a member of the Edinburgh police force. At present, he is lying wounded in an English hospital. On the 1st July, three of the pipers asked to be allowed to go forward with the men when the attack was launched. Anderson was hit shortly after crossing the parapet of the Royal Scots trench. He went on with the men notwithstanding his injury and on reaching the German trenches, he was hit a second time. About this time, he was attacked by one or more Germans.*

*What then happened was, in the words of one of the officers of the battalion, as follows – 'Throwing down his pipes, he went for the enemy with his fists, knocked one out, seized a rifle and joined in the fight. After that, he was lost sight of and we feared he had been killed, till we got word of him in a hospital with three or four wounds.'*

*The division of which the battalion formed a unit was awarded one Croix de Guerre and Anderson was selected for the honour, his being considered the most conspicuous case of gallantry. Every one of the officers and men who have received decorations, a correspondent states, has more than earned the honour awarded to them.*

In celebration of the anniversary of the Battle of Loos, a demonstration was held at the Mound, Edinburgh during the evening of Monday, 25 September. Piper Daniel Laidlaw VC, the King's Own Scottish Borderer's hero of the battle, stirred the large crowd of spectators with a selection of music played on the bagpipes. Several patriotic speeches were also delivered.

On Wednesday, 11 October, the police issued a warning to the public about a conman who had dressed in a soldier's uniform and visited the relatives of servicemen telling them that he had news of their loved ones.

**A game of bowls in progress at the Edinburgh War Hospital at Bangour. Nurses watch on and many of the men seem to have recovered well.**

**Mussels and periwinkles being cooked and sold in the High Street of Edinburgh during October 1916. The seller was said to have done a brisk trade with passers by.**

The man reportedly asked for money to pay for train fares so that he could obtain fuller information from the hospital in Edinburgh. The man wore the uniform of the Cameronians and police stated that several people had already been deceived by him.

On Friday, 13 October, it was reported that at a meeting of the Edinburgh Botanical Society, a proposal was made to list all members and remove the names of any known aliens.

The *Dundee Evening Telegraph* reported:

*In moving the motion, Sir Archibald Buchan Hepburn said that while those alien members had probably taken no individual part, at the same time they acquiesced by silence in the action of the leading scientific men, especially in Germany, and therefore they must bear the onus in common with their neighbours.*

*Mr Rutherford Hill, while not moving an amendment, asked if it were worth their while to push the matter, although he equally detested the methods of Prussianism.*

*The Very Rev. Dr Paul said that he was hampered in voting by not knowing how many alien members there were or who they were.*

*The secretary (Mr Smith) said that they were German and Austrian professors and leading botanists.*

*In reply to Mr Bennet Clark, the secretary said that there had been no communication from these alien members of any kind expressing disapproval of certain methods. There was no counter-proposal, the resolution was declared carried.*

On Tuesday, 17 October, the *Daily Record* reported a story about a private in the Scots Fusiliers:

*Private Thomas Cowe, awarded the Military Medal for carrying an important message under heavy shell and rifle fire and for bringing in his captain, who had been wounded, was a lamplighter in the employment of Edinburgh Corporation when he enlisted. His home is at 37 Milton Street, Edinburgh.*

The *Daily Record* of Thursday, 19 October reported that a sea lion in Edinburgh's Zoological Gardens had had a fight with two polar bears but survived the incident.

The same paper of Saturday, 21 October carried a story under the headline 'Lion-Feeder For The Army':

*Exemption was refused by the Edinburgh Local Tribunal yesterday in the case of a single man, 29 years of age, who feeds lions and other carnivorous animals in the Scottish Zoological Park at Corstorphine. The secretary of the Zoo urged the importance of a trustworthy employee being engaged on such work, as a bar or bolt on some of the cages might be left unfastened.*

On Saturday, 28 October, a flag day was held all over the country on behalf of the Naval and Military Veterans' Residence. In Edinburgh, a parade of veterans marched through the principal thoroughfares. Wearing scarlet tunics and Balmoral bonnets, the men were cheered as cars drove them through the streets. Military bands were also in attendance.

**A rest hut was added to the Edinburgh War Hospital at Bangour at the beginning of November. It had seating for 600 men. The photo shows some of the nurses and wounded soldiers in the grounds of the hospital.**

On Wednesday, 1 November, Lord Rosebery opened a branch of the Club for Overseas Soldiers at Ramsay Lodge on the Castlehill. There was a large attendance of Dominion troops and the event was presided over by the Marchioness of Linlithgow.

A shopkeeper wrote to the paper at the beginning of November complaining about the early closing hours imposed on himself and his fellow traders while ice-cream parlours remained open:

*I was rather surprised on coming down Leith Street and the Walk on Monday night, the first night of the early closing, to see all the ice-cream shops open. I understood they came under the same rule as other shops shutting at eight o'clock. Don't you think it is rather unfair that Edinburgh shopkeepers, such as confectioners and tobacconist and smallwares shops, must shut and yet a foreigner is allowed to keep open to 11, and opening at the time as others. I should like to know what Edinburgh shopkeepers think of this matter and if they are willing to allow it. Does it not seem like playing into foreigners' hands, as confectioners and tobacconists must shut at nine o'clock on Saturday and their customers, who are passing later in the evening and can't get their goods needn't bother, knowing they will get all they want in the ice-cream shops? No wonder it is becoming harder each year for Edinburgh shopkeepers to live when foreigners are allowed so much laxity in business matters.*

**The Marchioness of Linlithgow opened the rest hut at Edinburgh War Hospital at Bangour and spoke of the far-reaching effect of the work of the YMCA. Soldiers and nurses are pictured at the entrance to the hospital.**

On Saturday, 11 November, flag days were held in Edinburgh, Leith and Dundee in aid of war charities. A feature of the Edinburgh – Leith effort was a model yacht under the charge of a boy scout. Funds raised in the city went towards the British and Sailors Foreign Society.

Mr Lorne MacLeod was elected the new Lord Provost of Edinburgh during November. He replaced Lord Provost Sir Robert Inches.

On Thursday, 16 November, the *Edinburgh Evening News* carried a story under the headline 'Edinburgh Postman Arrested'. It read:

*An assistant postman named Walter Kidd Liddle (18) was remitted this morning from the Edinburgh City Police Court to the Burgh Court where he admitted a declaration on a charge under the Post Office Act. He is alleged to have stolen a packet containing two fountain pens and a registered packet containing 2s 6d and some stamps.*

On Thursday, 23 November, five boys appeared in the Edinburgh City Police Court on a charge of conducting themselves in a disorderly manner by shouting and bawling within an Edinburgh picture house. The boys were aged between 15 and 17 years old. It was stated that there had been two similar cases at the same picture house and, after a

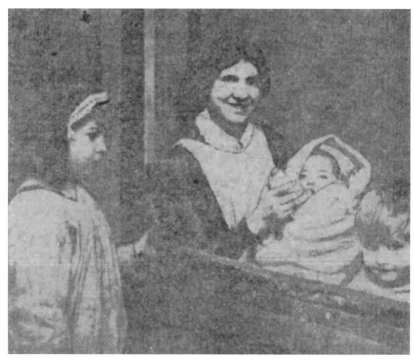

**A day nursery opened in Stockbridge, Edinburgh during November. The unit was for the children whose mothers were away doing vital war work. The Welfare of Children Committee set up the nursery which was able to care for 21 children at a time.**

conviction, there was a period of quietude. However, disturbances had soon broken out again. Bailie McArthy stated that conduct of this kind was very alarming in a dark picture house. He imposed fines of 10s, or seven days imprisonment, with £2 caution on each of the boys.

At the beginning of December, Grace Paterson Burke of Slateford Road, Edinburgh sued Edward Harvey, a wine and spirit merchant, for £500 for alleged seduction. The pursuer stated at the Court of Session that she was 21 years old and the defendant was about 50. It was recorded that in February 1915, she had been employed as a barmaid by the defendant and left in September. In the following April, she gave birth to a child and claimed the defendant was the father. The defendant denied seduction and paternity but as a settlement agreed to pay the pursuer £170 and expenses.

In the early hours of Tuesday, 19 December, the Edinburgh Express crashed on the Caledonian Railway near Carlisle. A guard, James Cameron, on board the goods train, was killed. The fireman onboard the postal train lost his arm in the incident which caused the engines to turn right around and the carriages to derail.

In the third week of December, a story appeared in the *Edinburgh Evening News* under the headline 'Tale About Husband Who Lost His Kit'. It read:

*"The effect of your conduct is to seal up people's charity," said Sheriff Orphoot in Edinburgh Sheriff Court today in passing sentence of two months' imprisonment on a woman named Mary Ellen Mellon for obtaining £2 18s by false pretences from ministers in Edinburgh, Corstophine and Colinton.*

*Her story to the people she victimised was that she resided in Belfast and that her husband was a soldier near that city. He had come to Edinburgh, she said, got drunk and lost his money and kit; he had wired to her to come from Belfast to help him out of his trouble and, after giving him her return ticket, she was left without any money. Thus she enlisted the sympathy of the people who she asked for money.*

During December, Sergeant Hugh McDonald, of the Highland Light Infantry, was awarded the Distinguished Conduct Medal for bravery in the field. He had enlisted at the outbreak of war and had been at the front for 19 months. He was previously employed by the Edinburgh and District Tramway Company at the Tollcross Depot.

Two pantomimes were performed in Edinburgh over the Christmas period. The Theatre Royal gave a lavish production entitled 'Red Riding Hood' while, at the King's Theatre, the seasonal panto was 'Cinderella'. Both attracted huge audiences and received excellent reviews.

The *Edinburgh Evening News* reported on the Waverley Carnival on Christmas Day:

*Between the gloom and the murk of the streets and the lighting and heating of the Waverley Market, there is these evenings a marked sense of contrast and it was no surprise to find the Carnival last night – there being, apparently, a good deal of "money to burn" in Edinburgh – a great place of rendezvous. Sailors, soldiers and civilians made up a great gathering and for one and all of the side shows and other attractions, there were thousands of patrons. "The Bombardment of Ypres", a remarkably realistic spectacle, the African Village, "The Beautiful Miss Okito", and other side shows each reaped a bountiful harvest and for such as took their entertainment on cheaper lines the platform performance was a great attraction. A number of the stage performers remain for a further term and among the new items are the Silbon performing cats, the Charley Meteor Trio in an aerial act and Spalding and Vangard, comedy acrobats.*

*Chapter Four*

# 1917 – Seeing it Through

On Friday, 5 January, reports appeared of a serious train crash near Edinburgh. Twelve people were killed and forty-three were injured. A passenger train leaving Waverley Station for Glasgow collided with a standing engine. The train was busy with passengers who were returning to Glasgow after the New Year holiday. Assistance was telephoned for and ambulances and cars hurried to the scene before the injured were taken to the Royal Infirmary in Edinburgh. Soldiers travelling on the train did their best to help the injured. Lance Corporal Radcliffe of the Royal Scots was interviewed by the *Aberdeen Weekly Journal* and said:

> *One officer in particular did awfully good work. He was worth ten of the other helpers. He was smashing everything to get into the imprisoned passengers in the first coach and he was still at it when I came away. I don't know what regiment he belonged to but he was a Scotsman anyway. I knew that by his tongue.*
>
> *There was a chap who I was carrying in who had his leg broken and was covered in blood. In spite of his serious injuries, he remarked cheerily, "We are not whacked yet." This poor fellow had just been, he told us, through at Edinburgh seeing his young son to the front.*

On Thursday, 18 January, it was reported that Edinburgh Town Council had unanimously adopted a resolution, passed by a conference of the six principal burghs in Scotland, in favour of the total prohibition of ardent spirits during the war and for the period of demobilisation. Representatives were reappointed for a further conference.

On Friday, 19 January, Edinburgh bakers protested against the licence, given by the new Order of Food controller, to millers to adulterate wheat flour with flour made from maize, barley, rice or oats. They regarded the proposal as injurious to the public interest and recommended instead that any licence to use flour, other than wheat flour in the making of bread, should be given to the makers of bread and be under their control.

On Tuesday 23 January, the *Aberdeen Express* reported a mysterious story under the headline 'An Edinburgh Myth':

*On investigation by the police, the story of the domestic servant who stated on Friday forenoon in Princes Street, Edinburgh, she was hustled into a taxi cab by two coloured men and taken as far as the Chocolate Works, Portobello, before she struggled free enough to open the cab door and fall on the street stunned, has been found to be a myth.*

Towards the end of January, the Carlton Hotel at North Bridge, Edinburgh was commandeered by the authorities to be used as government offices.

The *Daily Record* of Monday, 5 February carried a story about begging from soldiers:

*The practice of children begging from soldiers has become somewhat of a nuisance in Edinburgh of late and many complaints have been made especially by Colonials. In the City Police Court on Saturday, Bailie Inman ordered a boy, 13 years of age, to receive four strokes with the birch rod for the offence and he remarked that it was becoming too common and must be stopped.*

On the evening of Sunday, 11 February, four meetings were held in Edinburgh to further the War Loan. At the Empire Palace Theatre, Mr Munro, the secretary for Scotland, said that Germany would be watching the result of the loan. He said that by supporting the loan, people at home were supporting the army, navy and our allies.

At the Theatre Royal, the Lord Justice Clery said that just as they had astounded the world by the numbers of men they raised for the forces, they could also astound the world by the amount of money they raised for the loan. Lord Strathclyde spoke at the Palladium and said that they would raise a signal to the world to show that Britain means to see the conflict through to the end. Mr Parker MP also spoke at the meeting and Mr Clyde, Lord Advocate, spoke at the other meeting. All meetings were well attended.

On Wednesday, 21 February, the *Daily Record* reported a strange story under the heading 'A Kidnapping Hoax':

*For the second time within a few weeks, Edinburgh police have had reported to them a 'kidnapping' case which on investigation has proved to be a myth. On Monday morning, an eighteen-yea-old girl was found near Granton railway lying bound with ropes from head to foot. She related that about half-past five in the morning, two men wearing black cloaks and slouch hats had seized her in Granton Square and carried her off.*

*When interrogated by the police, however, she was ultimately led to admit that the story was a fabrication and that she herself had tied the ropes that bound her.*

Towards the end of February, the body of an Edinburgh soldier, Sergeant Thomas Blaikie, was found on rocks at the North Shore, Troon. He was a member of the Cameron Highlanders and had been attached to an Officers' Cadet Battalion. He had been missing since 16 February and it was not known how he had got into the water. He was 39 years of age and had served 21 years in the army.

At the beginning of March, a well-known Kingussie lady, Mrs Ronald Carswell, who was a superintending sister at the Edinburgh War Hospital in Bangour, was awarded the Royal Red Cross decoration. Both Mrs Carswell and her husband had come over from Canada so that they could do their bit to help the war effort.

**On 15 March, Nicholas II, the Russian Tsar, abdicated.**

The *Daily Record* of Friday, 16 March reported on the court proceedings against a female munitions worker:

*A girl of 18, who is in receipt of 14s 9d for a 52½ hours' week, was brought before the Edinburgh Munitions Tribunal yesterday on a charge of having absented herself from her work for a week. It was stated that she was a cotton-spinner with three years' experience, doing work of great national importance.*

*In reply to a question as to how the wage was so small if the girl was so expert, it was explained that the rate was fixed by the Ministry of Munitions. The headaches of which the girl complained would be relieved by an expenditure of 4s or 5s on a pair of glasses, which would take the strain off her eyes.*

*The chairman expressed the feeling of the court that if the firm wanted to help the girl, they should have the glasses supplied. It was also the feeling of the court that the wages were insufficient under the circumstances. Meantime the girl was ordered to return to work.*

On 24 March, the *Yellowstone News* in Montana carried the headline, 'U.S. Expected To Announce That State Of War Exists'. The newspaper went on to report that:

*News received from Plymouth that fifteen men, some of them Americans, had been drowned when the American merchantmen*

*Vigilancia* was sunk without warning by a German submarine.'

The story also stated:

> *President Wilson is expected, within 48 hours, to indicate definitely that he believes a virtual state of war exists between the United States and Germany.*

On Monday, 26 March, the *Dundee Evening Telegraph* published a letter from General Smuts to Lord Provost McLeod in Edinburgh. It read:

> *My Dear Lord Provost, Many thanks for your kind letter of welcome and for what you say about the intention to confer the freedom of your great city on me. Sir Robert Borden and I have agreed that we might go to Edinburgh on the same occasion. It is indeed a pleasure to me to find that what little I have been able to do during this great war has met with the approval of the citizens of Edinburgh.*

On Wednesday, 28 March, a meeting was held in Edinburgh in support of a fund to provide a permanent memorial to the men of the Canongate who had fallen in the war. Major Robertson VC, the chief recruiting officer in the city stated that 'No street in the Empire has done more for the Empire than the Canongate.'

On Wednesday, 4 April, it was reported that the agricultural section of the National Service Department of Scotland had been notified by the military authorities that they had agreed to an extension of agricultural furlough for soldiers working on the land. The military ploughmen had previously been sent to the Agricultural Depot, Tollcross School, Edinburgh before being dispatched to help farmers and were allowed to work up until 15 April but the extension meant that they would work on the land until the end of the month.

On 5 April, the *Evening Herald* reported:

> *The U.S. Senate has passed the resolution declaring a state of war with Germany by 82 votes to 6 at 11.15pm after 13 hours continuous debate. There was no demonstration when the result was announced.*

**America declared war on Germany on 6 April, 1917 in response to Germany's policy of unrestricted submarine warfare against Allied and neutral shipping.**

On Thursday, 12 April, the pensions minister, George Barnes MP, visited Edinburgh to attend a conference given by representatives of the local war pensions and disablement committees. Sir Arthur Griffith-Boscawen, who accompanied him, said that there were currently over 100,000 disabled soldiers and the figures were increasing all the time. It was expected that quarter of a million men would be eventually be receiving pensions of varying amounts.

Mr Barnes went on to make a statement about the treatment of the blind. He said that there should be a central register of each class of disablement. He continued that much had been done for limbless servicemen, more so than blinded servicemen who amounted to, he stated, approximately 630 men. Mr Barnes visited Newington House and was much impressed with the work done there.

On Friday, 13 April, the *Daily Record* carried a story of an Edinburgh boy's rescue:

*A thrilling story of the rescue of a boy from drowning is reported from Dunbar. It seems that the lad, who belongs to Edinburgh and was spending his Easter holiday in the town, had been amusing himself on the rocks below the cliffs at the west end of the burgh and had all means of escape cut off by the rapidly incoming tide.*

*His alarming plight was observed by a man who chanced to be walking along the cliffs and with all haste he proceeded to the shore for assistance.*

*Provided with ropes, a party of fishermen proceeded to the cliffs and, with a rope tightly secured around his waist, one of their number was lowered from the face of the cliffs, which are fully 100 feet above the sea level. The boy, who by this time, had climbed a few feet up the rugged cliff, was quickly secured by the fisherman and both of them were hauled to the summit of the Promenade.*

The amusing story of a German teacher's capture was reported in the *Edinburgh Evening News* of Saturday, 5 May:

*A weather-beaten soldier of a Lowland regiment, whose experience of the war was extensive, tells an interesting story. He had been with the first battalion of his regiment since Mons and had only been 13 days in Britain since the outbreak of war. He had been in all the big battles on the Western front and he thought the one now in progress was far and away the most successful.*

*"In every attack we made since Easter, my company has taken prisoners. Not long after I was wounded, a funny thing happened. A Fritz comes up to me and says, 'Hullo, Jock, how's your father?' I asked him who he was anyway and he said he'd been a schoolmaster in Edinburgh before the war. I marched him back*

*and the shells were pretty frequent. All the time, this Boche kept trying to hurry me up. 'Get a move on, Jock,' says he, 'or we'll never see Blighty.' He seemed to be very pleased at being captured."*

During May, Private John Marshall DCM, of the Seaforth Highlanders, received the Cross of St George from the Russian Government for distinguished services rendered in the field.

The story of a deserter's theft from an Edinburgh hotel was reported in the *Dundee Evening Telegraph* of Wednesday, 30 May. The article read:

*The story of how a soldier deserted his regiment to get married, and after that ceremony, on finding himself short of money, committed extensive hotel thefts, along with his bride, was told before Sheriff Neish at Dundee today.*

*Albert Cecil Stanley and Ann Henderson or Stanley, prisoners in Dundee prison, pleaded guilty to thefts from hotels in Edinburgh, Dysart and Kinghorn of jewellery and money to the value of £116.*

*Mr W.F. Mackintosh, the procurator-fiscal, explained that the male accuser was a deserter from the Royal Fusiliers, in which regiment he was a private. He was an Englishman but his wife was a native of Kirkcaldy, though she was a waitress in Edinburgh when he made her acquaintance.*

*In two of the hotels in which they have been lodging, they stole money and articles from the bedrooms of other guests. With regard to the Kinghorn hotel theft, they had only been in the place an hour for tea.*

*An agent, speaking on the accused's behalf, stated that the male accused deserted in order to get married, and after that ceremony the couple found themselves short of money and had committed the thefts.*

*Sheriff Neish sentenced Stanley to six months' imprisonment and his wife to two months.*

At the beginning of June, local newspapers reported the surprise meeting of a father and son at the front. Corporal Alexander Good, of the Scottish Rifles, who lived at 95 Canongate, Edinburgh and his son, Driver John Good, Royal Field Artillery, had both been at the front for two years when they met when the son's battery was passing by the place where his father's regiment was stationed. The father had been in the army for about three years and had fought at Loos. His daughter had unfortunately died since the two had last met.

Another story of a deserter appeared in the *Edinburgh Evening News* of Wednesday, 6 June:

*Private John Finlay, the soldier who, on Monday, kept the police at bay for five hours from the roof of a house in Cambridge Road, Norbiton was brought up at the police court yesterday. He was charged with being a deserter from a Training Reserve Battalion at Edinburgh and, after formal evidence, he was remanded to await an escort.*

On Tuesday, 19 June, it was reported that Bombardier Norman J. Burnett, Royal Garrison Artillery, had been awarded the Military Medal. He was the youngest son of Mr and Mrs Burnett of 11 Grindlay Street, Edinburgh and was just 21 when the medal was awarded.

With their fathers away at war, many children found themselves up to mischief. A story appeared in the *Edinburgh Evening News* of Saturday, 23 June under the headline 'Youthful Housebreakers':

*Anthony Campbell (12), James Parkinson (11) and John Price (11), all residing at 212 Canongate, Edinburgh, were charged with three acts of housebreaking. Campbell and Parkinson were charged with breaking into the Old Kirk, St John Street, Edinburgh and stealing from a lockfast box there 7s 3d in money. The whole three were further charged with breaking into a shoe repairing company's premises in Chalmers' Close and stealing 19s 7d of money, a wristlet and a watch and Campbell and Price were also charged with breaking into a lockfast desk and stealing 13s of money. They all pleaded guilty. The method adopted had been to break glass and crawl through the hole which they had made. In connection with a second charge, on a desk on the premises on which they had entered, they left a note on which was written, "Done by the two methylated spirits' drinkers, Tom and Pat."*

*It was stated by Mr McLean for the defence that none of the boys had been in trouble before and that their mothers had known nothing of the occurrences, until the mother of the first boy had found the watch in her house and immediately taken it to the lost property office when the thefts were revealed.*

*Bailie Buchan said there was something seriously defective in the system under which these children were being trained that they saw cases of this kind, of young boys committing these serious offences with no apparent sense of the wrong done. He sentenced each to receive 12 stripes of the birch rod.*

Viscount French visited Edinburgh on 23 June to present a number of war decorations. A mother can be seen in the photo collecting the medal of her son who was killed in battle.

A grand march past took place on 23 June and Viscount French can be seen taking the salute from the Royal Scottish Academy galleries in Edinburgh. Shown in the picture are (left to right): Viscount French, Major General H.S. Gardiner, Lord Provost Sir J. MacLeod, General Sir J. Spencer Ewart, Sir George McCrae and Mr Harry Rawson, the chairman of the Territorial Force Association.

At the beginning of July, the Allotments Sub-Committee of Edinburgh Council received a communication from the Board of Agriculture saying that it was vital that potatoes within allotments were sprayed to ensure the preservation of the crop. The committee agreed to instruct Mr McHattie to purchase three machines which could be used for the spraying. The machines were costly at over £100 each and it was stated that this would have to be paid by the allotment owners. However, with the amount of allotment holders in the city, the cost was considerably lightened for each person.

On 3 July, the Victoria League in Edinburgh marked the occasion of Canada Day by supplying entertainment to 130 wounded Canadian soldiers from various hospitals in the city and district. Canadian soldiers on furlough also attended. The men were given dinner and tea and were also provided with cigarettes.

The contributions to the Edinburgh Red Cross Fund in the first week

**Fair holiday scenes on the Scottish coast during July 1917. Happy swimmers take a quick dip while watched by many curious spectators.**

of July amounted to £763 making the overall total of £100,374. Sir Thomas Beecham's Opera Company donated £200 from various performances in the city.

At Edinburgh City Police Court on the morning of Thursday, 5 July, Bailie McArthy disposed of ten cases. The charges were: Incapable and breach of the peace, three each; loitering, two; drunk in charge of a horse and housebreaking, one each.

The *Edinburgh Evening News* of Saturday, 7 July told of a court appearance for a man dealing in exemption certificates:

> *Patrick Docherty, a middle-aged man, was remitted yesterday from Glasgow to the High Court at Edinburgh on a charge under the Defence of the Realm Act of procuring and supplying, on five occasions, altered or irregular classification certificates entitling the persons holding them to exemption from military service in respect that they had been medically rejected and the signature of each of which was forged. He pleaded guilty to three of the charges.*

**Delighted Edinburgh children paddle during the fair holiday. Travelling to the seaside was a treat from many youngsters from larger cities.**

An aviation exhibition began in Edinburgh on 20 July. It was opened by Lady Beatty and took place in the College of Art, Lauriston Place. The proceeds of the funds collected as admission charges were donated to local hospitals especially those which looked after wounded aviators. The exhibits included all kinds of aircraft, Zeppelin wreckage and the machine of the late Flight Sub Lieutenant Reginald Warneford VC. Also on show were the last enemy machines brought down in France by

**Edinburgh citizens taking a dip in the sea during the fair holiday while a man in a suit looks after their clothes and towels.**

**Happy bathers pose for the camera while in the surf at Girvan during the fair holiday in July.**

Captain Albert Ball VC and one of the Albatross type, fitted with a 160hp Mercedes engine.

The Countess of Drogheda, who organised the event, lent her large collection of air prints and paintings covering aerial flight through the ages. It was said to be the largest collection of such material anywhere. A large number of photographs gave a complete summary of aircraft history. The Countess was the only female member of the Aeronautical Society Council. The event continued until 3 August.

On 23 July Siegfried Sassoon, the war poet, was admitted to Craiglockhart Hydropathic which was used as a psychiatric hospital for shell-shocked officers returning from the front. Patients were treated there between 1916 and 1919. Many poets and writers were amongst them including Wilfred Owen and Robert Graves. Owen and Sassoon arrived at the hospital in 1917 and were subsequently, after treatment, returned to the war. Owen died on 6 November 1918, just five days before the Armistice.

**The Battle of Passchendaele began on 31 July. It was also known as the Third Battle of Ypres.**

On Monday, 6 August, the trial took place at Edinburgh of Joseph

**Edinburgh's gas-propelled bus made an appearance in the city during July 1917. The bag on the top of the bus carried enough gas to feed the engine during the round trip of fifteen miles between Edinburgh and Loanhead.**

Wilmot. He was charged with murdering his wife and two young children at their home in the city. The defendant pleaded not guilty and the court was told that he was insane at the time. The evidence stated that

**The Marchioness of Linlithgow opening the veterans' fete at the Grange Grounds in Edinburgh on 21 July. On her right is Lord Strathclyde who addressed the crowd.**

**The Earl of Selborne talking at the Highland and Agricultural Society of Scotland's conference on the approval of agriculture in Edinburgh on 9 August. Also seen in the photo are the Marquis of Linlithgow, Dr Douglas and the secretary of the society.**

Wilmot, who had once been in the army, had suffered from melancholia caused by his inability to work due to locomotor ataxy, an inability to control bodily movements. On the night in question, he attacked his family with a hammer before fleeing to Glasgow intending to drown himself. However, he later handed himself into the police who broke into his home and found the bodies.

The jury found that Wilmot was insane at the time and he was ordered to be detained at His Majesty's Pleasure.

On 11 August, the Royal Blind Asylum and School appealed for urgent funds to 'meet the pressing needs of the blind industrial workers.' Subscriptions were to be sent to the Treasurer at 58 Nicolson Street, Edinburgh.

A letter from a reader appeared in the *Edinburgh Evening News* of Wednesday 15 August under the headline 'A Touching Tram Incident':

*In a car the other day, I witnessed a touching act by one of the women conductors. A rather poorly clad woman, not looking well, with a baby of from three to four months old, tendered a penny for a ticket. The conductress bent over her and whispered and asked her if she was a soldier's wife. The passenger said yes and the conductress gave her hand a squeeze and handed her back her penny and a ticket. I was sitting next to the soldier's wife with the baby and the little incident just about bowled me out. I forgot to say that I asked the conductress of the car if she was a soldier's wife. She smiled sweetly and said, "No such luck. I am single."*

A young man's career of crime appeared in the *Edinburgh Evening News* of Tuesday, 21 August:

*A young man, named Lawrence Hardwick, appeared before Sheriff Guy at Edinburgh Sheriff Court today in answer to several charges of theft. On 31st July, he was charged with breaking into the Young Men's Guild hut at Portobello and stealing a quantity of biscuits, chocolates, tobacco, matches, pencils and soap. A further charge bore that on the 7th inst. accused broke into an office in Newington Road, occupied by a coal merchant, and there stole four letters containing bank cheques of the value of £152 10s, a revolver and case, a ring, pocket-book purse and 8s.*

*Accused pleaded guilty to the charges and there were libelled against him convictions for theft at Bradford, Preston and Liverpool, while the last was at Edinburgh Sheriff Court, where, in February last, accused got six months and was just out of prison at the beginning of this month. Hardwick appeared in the uniform of a Scottish regiment but Sheriff Guy said that he had apparently been released from the Borstal Institution at Liverpool to join the Army. It had apparently been a mistake to take the accused into the Army. The sentence would be one of 12 months imprisonment.*

At the beginning of September, the Committee of the Argyll and Sutherland Highlanders Prisoners of War Fund gratefully accepted a sum of £595 9s 5d which was the proceeds of a cricket match played at the Grange Ground, Edinburgh. The event was organised by the officers of the Argyll and Sutherland Highlanders. Private Fulton organised an organ recital which raised £10 4s in aid of the fund and 11s was raised by No 7 Company of the Girl Guides.

During the previous month, 2,316 parcels had been dispatched to the prisoners and 1,101 acknowledgements had been received.

One prisoner of war wrote:

*Minden, Germany.*

*Dear Madam,*

*I take the pleasure of writing this letter in answer to your nice letter, so I hope you received the postcards I send to you. I am pleased to see that you have still to do with the parcels, and I must say that everything that I have sent for I have got all right. I have just received the shaving kit I asked for, and I am well pleased with*

*it. We are getting the parcels more regular and the food that comes in the parcels is always welcome. We have found out that the parcels through the Committee is a good arrangement, as everything comes in good condition and well packed, and the postcard inside of them which to answer them with, which I like to send away as soon as I get them to let the donors know that I am getting them safely. I must draw to a close thanking you and the donors for the trouble you are taking over us, sending the parcels out to us which is ever welcome.*
*Yours sincerely*

*N. McLeod, Argyll and Sutherland Highlanders.*

The Edinburgh Municipal Comforts Committee commenced operations for the winter during the month of September. On 13 September, Bailie Watson, the acting secretary, dispatched 44 bales and cases to France and Egypt. These contained 2,100 socks, 48 shirts, 250 mufflers, 200 books for hospitals and a number of miscellaneous articles. The committee's work had been highly appreciated in the past and they intended to carry on supplying men at the front with the comforts that they needed. An appeal was due to be issued for help to carry on the work and they were expecting a warm response from the public.

A large quantity of wool had been purchased by the committee before

**A gathering in the city in October in memory of the men who fell at Loos. A huge crowd watched the event. Pictured are: Mr R Munro, secretary for Scotland; the Reverend J. McLean Watt; Lord Provost Sir J. Lorne MacLeod; Colonel Mackay; Colonel Critchton-Browne; Reverend J. Black and Lieutenant Colonel Robertson VC.**

the heavy rise in price took place. This was to be offered free to work parties in the city for the purpose of knitting socks and other articles.

On Tuesday, 18 September, Edinburgh town council unanimously agreed that the freedom of the city should be conferred on the American ambassador, Walter Hines Page. This was in recognition of his representative position, his public gifts and his services in promoting friendship between the United States and Great Britain.

A soldier's wife wrote to the *Edinburgh Evening News* on Saturday, 6 October saying:

> *With the winter facing us now, when there is extra fire needed, is it not time poor Tommy's wife and dependants were receiving some more attention? It seems harder to live as time goes on. In fact, I am nearly distracted trying to make ends meet. Out of my £1 4s 6d this week, I have paid 18s 6d for boots for the two boys. Last week was rent week and that was £1. The children require warm garments for winter. In God's name, how long are we to be kept in this hand-to-mouth state? It is time now that we were getting fair play. How I envy the American soldier's wife!*

On Wednesday, 10 October, a fine of £10 was imposed on an alien, who had formerly been living in Edinburgh, after he was caught stealing soap. Augustus Charles Huber, aged 54 and working as a photographer, was found guilty of the offence which took place in Glasgow. He was Austrian by birth and had left Edinburgh for Glasgow after the former city had been made a prohibited area for enemy aliens.

A letter appeared in the *Edinburgh Evening News* of Saturday, 13 October complaining about the poorly lit streets:

> *I think it is disgraceful to have the north part of the town in total darkness. In going home on Thursday night, as it was raining, I had my umbrella up, and in going down Duke Street, owing to the darkness, I had gradually got to the edge of the pavement where I fell on my knees and got bruised on several places. There are a few steps leading to the roadway not easily seen. What can be the object of having several parts of the town entirely dark and other parts well lit? If a raid were made, does it not stand to reason that they would operate on the bright places instead of a partly lighted thoroughfare. I trust something will be done. Otherwise there may be more serious accidents.*

It was reported in October that 10,000 houses of four apartments would be required to meet the needs of Edinburgh at the end of the war. Lord

**Dr Page, the American Ambassador, visiting the Lincoln statue in the old Carlton burial ground in Edinburgh on 2 November. Afterwards, he received the Freedom of the City from dignitaries in the Usher Hall before being presented with an honorary degree in the McEwan Hall.**

Provost Sir J. Lorne MacLeod stated that Edinburgh Town Council felt that there was a great need for further housing accommodation within the city for the working classes and asked the local Government Board for public funds so that the work could be carried out.

Mr Stevenson, who seconded the motion, expressed the view that this would be the first step towards a great scheme of much needed housing reform within the city.

## On 7 November, the Bolsheviks successfully overthrew the Russian government.

An advert appeared in the *Edinburgh Evening Express* of Saturday, 10 November complete with a topical rhyme:

'Now Tom is back at work, one-armed,
The changes make him quite alarmed;
For ladies at his table sit,
And flappers smile from opposite;
The girls perform his pre-war tasks,
And tell him things before he asks.
They make his tea and take his bets,
And bring him Chairman cigarettes.
Said Tom, 'The modern style is bliss,
A married Turk's a fool to this!'

On Saturday, 17 November, a reader wrote a letter to the *Edinburgh Evening News* about further recruitment. It read:

*I see Sir Auckland Geddes is calling for more men for the army and that there is more "talk" of a big "comb-out". I am interested in this, for I am already in the army, have been for the past three years, and now want to get out of it as quickly as possible. Now this gentleman was, previous to his present appointment, Director of Recruiting at the War Office, and he knows, for he is no fool, that there are thousands of men already in the army who are at the present moment simply being wasted. He is indexing the army at home and is apparently going to stop there. Couldn't he also index the army behind the army in France, where category A are safely ensconced? We certainly have heard a good deal about wounded men and men unfit for active service being placed in the cushy jobs behind the lines but, alas, it is seldom that we hear that such a procedure is being adopted. The authorities know this and simply wink their eye at it.*

*Officers who have been wounded once, twice or three times are regularly sent back to the front as soon as passed fit, while others, who are on the 'Permanent Establishment' of their units, such as adjutant assistants, fit for general service, for which, incidentally, they receive 5s per day extra duty pay, are allowed to remain at home on the representation of their commanding officers that they are indispensable and that the "interests of the service" would suffer if they were replaced. And all the while, the cry rings out "more men, more men". The "more men" are often found from the weak and the maimed; many of the fit are allowed to remain in their cushy jobs.*

On Thursday, 29 November, in the hall of the Barclay United Free Church in Edinburgh, special and regular constables entertained 220 wounded soldiers to tea. The men were conveyed to the hall by motor bus and came from five hospitals in the division. They were given tea as well as gifts of tobacco, cigarettes and chocolate. After tea, a concert was given by well-known local artistes.

**On 17 December, an armistice agreed between Russia and the Central Powers came into effect.**

The Christmas pantomimes in the city included 'Jack and the Beanstalk' at the King's Theatre and 'Humpty Dumpty' at the Theatre Royal. Miss Lily Morris appeared as Jack at the King's Theatre and got a standing ovation from the audience who had joined in with many of the songs she sang. Fred Dupres and Nellie Wallace provided much of the comedy in the production.

In 'Humpty Dumpty', Ray Holgate played the nursery boy and comedians George Jackley and Tom Newell provided much of the fun.

The Christmas celebrations in the city were reported in the *Edinburgh Evening News* of Tuesday, 25 December:

*The weather is delightful, with a slight touch of frost and a clear*

**The funeral of Dr Elsie Inglis took place on 29 November. The cortege can be seen coming down the Mound from St Giles', where a service was held before proceeding to Princes Street. Large crowds gathered to show their respect.**

*bracing air, making an ideal Christmas Day so far as climatic conditions are concerned. There is evidence in most of the streets that as a holiday, Christmas is more and more coming to be observed. In the principal streets, nearly all the shops were closed and others, which were not closed for the whole of the day, closed for the half, a number making their half-holiday today instead of tomorrow. Another departure becoming increasingly prominent is the holding of church services.*

*This year, several entertainments, which used to be given at this time, have been discontinued. One donor who for years had given this to the inmates of the poorhouse regretfully intimating that, owing to the present conditions, he thought the usual treat was out of place. No doubt, too, the advices of the Food Director to avoid all waste and to economise has had its effect and these feast days which bulked so largely in the lives of the recipients have been discontinued. There are still, however, a few remaining but these are mostly concerned with children and the military hospitals.*

*The experience of merchants is that the season has been one of*

**The burial in Edinburgh of Dr Elsie Inglis who was the founder of Scots Women's Hospitals. Crowds gathered at Dean Cemetery in the city to visit her grave.**

*the best they have experienced. In some trades, a record has been reached in the way of purchases for Christmas presents especially in the jewellery and fancy goods trade.*

On Christmas Day, a party of 100 Edinburgh boys and girls, under the charge of Councillor Barrie of the Grassmarket Mission, left the Mound on buses during the morning bound for the Forth. There, they were the guests of the crew of an American warship. It was the custom on American ships to give Christmas treats to children. Not only were the children entertained, but a number of them were given new clothes. The sum of £70 was raised to fit out the boys. There was much merriment and every child also received a toy.

A letter from a mother appeared in the *Edinburgh Evening News* of Wednesday, 26 December. It read:

*Certainly it is time mothers spoke out for their martyr sons who go so bravely to fight a man's battle. So many able-bodied men, who have had their day and pleasure, are chuckling that they are just over the age and content their conscience with the stock phrase that 'it is a young man's war' Cowards, all of them! Let the Government take a census and see how many of these darlings of*

**Captain Henry Reynolds VC MC (Royal Scots) who became known as 'The Pill-Box Hero.' He was given an enthusiastic welcome on his arrival at Edinburgh's Princes Street station on 26 December. Shown pictured are Mr Harry Rawson, chairman of the Edinburgh Territorial Association, Sir J.H.A MacDonald and Captain Reynolds and his wife and children.**

*over 41 have offered their services and see if it is not time they raised the age instead of taking our boys of 17. If the women had had the vote, such cruelty would never have been talked about. I am a mother of nine children. Three sons have served their country. One died a hero. I have one now 17 years and still the Government will take him if matters go on. It is for the men of our country to show what they are made of and demonstrate a bit instead of being fireside talkers. Never will this war be won while the slaughter of innocent youth continues. Men of 42, take your stand and save the youth of the country.*

On Thursday, 27 December, the *Daily Record* reported the arrival of Captain Henry Reynolds of the 12th Royal Scots in Edinburgh who was invalided home due to wounds that he had received in action. Captain Reynolds was awarded the Victoria Cross for his heroic exploits on 20 September 1917 near Frezenberg, Belgium. He earned the name 'The Pill-Box Hero' because he was honoured for his capturing of four pill-boxes while leading an advance into enemy territory. A large crowd met him at Princes Street station and there was much cheering and hand shaking.

*Chapter Five*

# 1918 – The Final Blows

On Tuesday, 1 January, the *Daily Record* recorded the holiday atmosphere in the city on the previous day:

> *There was a distinct holiday spirit manifest in Edinburgh yesterday. A large number of people came in from the country districts and Princes Street was thronged during the afternoon. The places of amusement were well patronised and at the theatres the booking lists were all taken up. At the Tron Church, the usual large crowd watched the passing of the hour at midnight.*

During January 1918, sugar was rationed. By the end of April, meat, butter, margarine and cheese were also rationed. Ration cards were issued and people were required to register with their local butcher and grocer. People in Edinburgh joined long queues to get the basic of foods including potatoes and many other vegetables.

**The war bond tank was brought to Edinburgh by a special train on 6 January and took up its place facing Princes Street. The tank, *Julian*, had been a phenomenal success in other parts of the country and attracted huge crowds.**

**An enormous crowd gathered in Princes Street waiting to purchase war bonds and war saving certificates from the Tank during January 1918.**

The *Edinburgh Evening News* of Thursday, 10 January carried the news of the city's Tank Week. The story read:

*Today is proving the big day, so far as the week at the Mound has gone, not in regard to the amount of money invested, but in volume of traffic. It will be a day of queues. They had formed by ten o'clock and an hour later, they had the all too restricted area in what looked, to the casual passer-by, a state of dire confusion. There was a War Bond queue and a War Savings Certificate queue and a Maule prize fund queue and a £1,000 free gift scheme queue.*

*Yesterday, War Savings Certificates to the value of over £30,000 were purchased, a record, it is believed, for all Tank Banks anywhere. Today that figure should be eclipsed. Why, at half past ten o'clock, the Certificates queue had its head in one of the booths and its tail in Princes Street, hugging the railing that fences off East Princes Street Gardens.*

*Having regard to the growing strength of the queues, it was nothing short of a mercy that the weather conditions continued*

**The Lord Provost standing on top of Julian, the Tank Bank, on 8
January. It was an overcast day but people still turned out in their
thousands and gave him an enthusiastic welcome.**

> *fine. It was cold, of course, but the breeze had not the bitterness of
> the first two days of the week and if there was a long wait – one
> man who lined up at half past ten drew 'no prize' a little before 12
> o'clock – there was always a great deal of coming and going and
> the distraction of a military band, together, at midday, with the
> usual speechmaking from the top of the Tank.*

On Thursday, 17 January, the *Edinburgh Evening Express* reported on
the frosty weather in the city. A great increase in burst pipes was noted
and in one tenement, there were over thirteen bursts. People leaving their

water taps running, hoping to stop pipes from breaking, cause further blockages when the water later froze elsewhere in the pipes. The Sanitary Department in the city endeavoured to clear them quickly but were hampered by the lack of plumbers.

On Thursday, 7 February, three conmen appeared in court. The story was carried in the *Edinburgh Evening News*:

*At the Edinburgh City Police Court today, John Charles Steuart, Thomas Wood and Joseph Wood pleaded not guilty to a charge on February 1, in the carriage of a train travelling between Edinburgh and Kirkcaldy, they, being card-sharpers, induced two soldiers to engage in an unlawful game known as the 'three-card trick' and cheated them of £17.*

*One of the soldiers, a rifleman in the New Zealand Forces, in the witness-box, said that he and his brother were going to Dundee and at the Waverley Station, when looking for a seat, Steuart and Wood said to come into their carriage as there was plenty of room. Thomas Wood than came into the carriage. When the train passed Haymarket Station, Joseph Wood offered to show them the three-card trick but he said the charge would be 2s 6d all round. No one offered to pay 2s 6d but he said that as they were a good-looking lot, he would show them the trick for nothing. After a time, Wood asked the witness to put a 'fiver' on and he lost it. The witness then went on betting until he had lost £9 and his brother £8.*

*Just before the train came to stop at Kirkcaldy, the accused had a row among themselves about the turning up of the cards at the wrong time. When the train stopped, witness said that all the accused went out and witness became suspicious. When the ticket inspector came round, witness remarked that they had been "done down for £17." The inspector said witness should have told him they were on the train. When they returned to Edinburgh, they reported the matter.*

*Cross-examined by Mr John Robertson, solicitor for the accused, as to whether witness was cheated, he said yes. Accused's agent suggested that witness was not cheated but was unlucky.*

Lord Provost Sir J. Lorne McLeod spoke at the evening meeting of the Holyrood Garden Allotments Association on Friday, 8 February. He stated that due to the large demand for allotments in the city, arrangements had been made for 50 more to come into use making a total of 106. At the same meeting, Mr J.W. McHattie, the city gardener, delivered an informative lecture on what to grow and how to grow it.

The staff of the Fountainbridge School Cooking Centre preparing cheap meals for the people of Edinburgh under the city's scheme of communal feeding.

On Monday, 11 February, the main recruitment office in Edinburgh opened in the Music Hall in George Street. It covered all areas of the city as well as Peebles and Lothians.

**On 3 March, Russia signed a peace treaty with the Central Powers known as the Treaty of Brest-Litovsk.**

On Wednesday, 13 March, the Lord Provost's Committee suggested

**The American Club was opened in Edinburgh on 23 February by the secretary of Scotland. At the front of the photo can be seen the lieutenant who was in charge of the American soldiers who attended the ceremony.**

bestowing the honour of Freedom of the City on the Right Honourable David Lloyd George MP in recognition of his many services to the state.

The readers of the *Edinburgh Evening Herald* on Wednesday, 27 March responded to an article about lax morals in the city. 'Jus' wrote:

*I pass up and down Leith Street and though I have seen many girls and fellows speaking to one another, I cannot say I have seen the same disorderly scenes that your correspondent writes about.*

'SN' wrote:

*There is nothing out of place or immodest in a girl taking an interest in a soldier. It would be better, perhaps, if more followed their example.*

'An Auld Reekie Girl' wrote:

*Just a word to the girls. Go in for fun! Certainly enjoy yourselves while you are young. You will be old soon enough. But don't let your love of fun carry you over the line of ladylike conduct, beyond dignity and self-respect. Give the boys a good time if you have the chance. They deserve it; but don't let them go back 'down under' with a bad impression of Auld Reekie girls. Meanwhile, is every church in Edinburgh doing its level best to help these stranger soldiers to enjoy their spare time?*

**On 21 March the German Spring Offensive – the Kaiser's Battle – began on the Western Front forcing the British and French armies to retreat.**

Towards the end of March, it was noticed that there was an increase in recruitment within the city. Experienced officials said that it was reminiscent of the beginning of the war. A number of volunteers registered at the offices at the Music Hall and amongst them were several men who had been discharged from the army and men who were over age but who had served a long period of service in France. The men weren't re-enlisting for home service but wanted to return to France to fight. A well-known sergeant in the city suggested that a series of recruitment drives would bring in hundreds of men who were vitally needed overseas.

Edinburgh's morality again featured in the *Aberdeen Journal* of Friday, 29 March:

*Outstanding features of the annual report for 1917, which has been issued by Chief Constable Ross, Edinburgh, are the slight decrease of criminal prosecutions compared with the previous year, the decrease in certain forms of juvenile crime, and the greatly decreased number of arrests for drunkenness. There was also a considerable decrease in the number of women arrested on charges of prostitution, which the Chief Constable contributes entirely to the greater demand for female labour and that many of these women have taken the opportunity of seeking useful employment. The number arrested during the year was 278, a decrease of 116.*

On Friday, 5 April, Edinburgh's Aeroplane Week was announced which was to run from 8–13 April. On Monday, 8 April, it was announced that the city was aiming to provide aeroplanes for the war at an expenditure of £1,000,000. A formal ceremony was held at Waverley Market where there were photographs of British aircraft both at home and serving in France. A military band played at the event which was presided over by the Lord Provost. He stated that the first million pounds had already been secured and the object was to secure a second million which would greatly help in bringing the war to an end.

On Tuesday, 9 April, the Edinburgh Licensing Court met and stated that the closing time for licensed premises had been set at 10pm. However, in fourteen cases, the regulation had been breached with owners permitting 'treating' on the premises.

On Thursday, 11 April, the widespread recall of men who had previously been exempted was announced. Known as a 'comb out' the plan was to enlist men in the army straightaway who had previously been classed as exempt, in luxury professions or too old. Every man in categories A, B1 or C1, born in or after the year 1875, was to be immediately called up.

This was the day that Sir Douglas Haig, Commander-in-Chief of the British Army, issued his famous 'Backs to the Wall' order of the day: 'There is no other course open to us but to fight it out. Every position must be held to the last man: there must be no retirement. With our backs to the wall and believing in the justice of our cause each one of us must fight on to the end. The safety of our homes and the Freedom of mankind alike depend upon the conduct of each one of us at this critical moment.'

The Edinburgh Spring Holiday was written about in the *Evening News* on Monday, 15 April:

*After a bitterly cold weekend, the weather was slightly milder, if dull, for the Edinburgh spring holiday. Practically all shops were closed, including licensed premises. A good many people took advantage of the holiday to make short trips into the country but there was practically no long-distance travelling. Picnic parties to Portobello and the Pentlands accounted for a number of holidaymakers, while the motor buses starting from the Waverley Bridge to places in the neighbourhood were greatly patronised.*

The *Edinburgh Evening News* of Thursday, 18 April carried a story under the headline 'Hotel Manager Seriously Assaulted'. It read:

*Before Bailie Malcolm Stuart at the Edinburgh City Police Court today, Archibald Elder (30), waiter, 78 Brunswick Street, pleaded guilty to having assaulted the assistant manager of a hotel. Accused had been drunk and the manager, on remonstrating with him, was seriously assaulted. The magistrates fined him £5 or 30 days imprisonment.*

During May, the local newspaper carried a report about the oldest Indian Army veteran in the city. Lieutenant Colonel Andrew Aytoun, of the Royal Artillery, the oldest Indian officer in Scotland, had died at his residence, 28 Inverleith Row, Edinburgh. He was 93 years of age. He was the son of Mr James Aytoun and the cousin of Professor Aytoun, the poet. In 1844 he went to India and served in the local conflicts there. He returned to India after the outbreak of the Mutiny and took part in the suppression. Subsequently, he was engaged by the Indian government in geological survey work.

On Friday, 17 May, the *Edinburgh Evening Express* reported the assault on an American sailor:

*In Edinburgh City Police Court today, Richard Letton pleaded not guilty before Bailie Adams to a charge that on 15th May, he assaulted Marshall David Hamner, a fireman in the American Navy, by striking him on the face.*

*In the course of his evidence, Hamner stated that he was walking around the town with a friend when he met the accused and a another man. The accused offered to get them some whisky, and witness agreed and said he would pay for it. The accused took them to a stair in a side street and having been given 9s from witness he went to a house while witness and friend waited. The accused returned with a bottle. "We had been done before", said witness, so we decided to sample the bottle right there, and when we did we found that it was water. We demanded our money back, and the accused returned it. We then returned to the main thoroughfare and the accused came with us. He then insulted me by saying that Americans were fools for not knowing the difference between water and whisky. I then hit out at him, but missed him, and then I fell, and he hit me over the eye with a knuckle-duster, or something like it in his hand. Accused then ran off. I took my pocket-knife out when I chased him, but could not catch him."*

*The witness stated that he would very likely have used the knife if he had caught the accused. It was not the American way to let a man hit you and run away without trying to get some of your own back. (laughter). Fireman Welsh, who was a fellow ship mate of Hamner's, and was described as pure-bred American Indian, said the bottle accused offered was just coloured water, when his "pard" hit out at the accused he missed him because the "guy's" face did not happen to be there, (laughter). Cross-examined as to what Hamner would have done with the knife if he had caught the accused, Welsh replied, "I reckon he would have got to work on him with it".(loud laughter). The accused in his evidence maintained that Hamner struck him first, and he merely acted in self-defence. When Hamner drew the knife he had to run for his life.*

*Bailie Adams, in finding the charge proved, said the sailors had given a straightforward account of what happened. Being unaccustomed to our laws they did not probably know that the whisky transaction was wrong, and they were incensed when the accused called them fools. He imposed a fine of £5 or 30 days' imprisonment.*

In the third week of May, a new scheme came into place with regard to food rationing in the city. Application forms were issued through the post office in Edinburgh which covered all people living in the household or establishment, including lodgers and all persons who may be temporarily absent from the household. Children away at boarding school had to be included in the application for their home. Temporary visitors were not included, if they had already made applications elsewhere.

It was the duty of each householder to fill in the name of any person who was entitled to a supplementary ration card and information regarding adolescent boys between the age of 13 and 18. Information was also required in respect of persons receiving supplies from farmers or other food producers. The ration book covered sugar, fats (butter or margarine), meat and tea. The public had to take steps to register with their respective suppliers and the registration had to be with the retailer from whom the householder is at present getting his supplies.

On Wednesday 22 May, the Duke of Atholl, the Lord High Commissioner, visited Newington Hotel for Blinded Soldiers and Sailors in Edinburgh and conveyed a message to the men from the king telling them that His Majesty intensely admired the plucky way in which they were meeting their difficulties and that they had played their game well in the past and that he was sure they would continue in the same spirit.

On Thursday, 30 May a special scale of rationing was announced by the Scottish Local Government Food Board, which had been arranged with the Ministry of Food for tuberculosis and fever patients in hospitals and for tuberculosis patients living at home. Applications were to be made to the local Food Control office.

Towards the end of May, the *Edinburgh Evening News* carried a story under the headline 'Children's Meat Rations'. It read:

*Edinburgh food control committee have completed the scheme for giving extra meat rations to all children in the city between six and ten years, as well as boys from 13 to 18. About 40,000 cases were involved. An appeal was made for the aid of the staffs of the schools, and that appeal met with the most cordial response. Through their instrumentality the scheme has been carried through without a hitch.*

An advert appeared in the *Edinburgh Evening News* of Saturday, 1 June requesting second-hand bagpipes. A Royal Scots soldier, writing from a Red Cross Hospital, said that he was desirous of getting a set of bagpipes of his own and not being able to purchase a new set would like to put in a communication with some one who would sell him a second-hand set in good condition. He expected to be in Edinburgh shortly and any offer sent to the newspaper would be sent on to the Royal Scot.

In the city's newspaper of Saturday, 8 June, an article appeared under the headline 'Edinburgh University in Wartime':

*Probably more than most of the institutions of the Scottish capital the University can claim to have been profoundly affected by war conditions. Numerically the position is almost startling. In the session 1913-14, towards the end of which, as the academic year runs, the war commenced, there were 3,283 matriculated students. In the following year the number had fallen to 2,417. But in the year 1915-16 there were only 1,811, or not much more than half of the number of two years before. In 1916-17 there was a slight revival to 1,887, while in 1917-18, up to the end of April last, there were 1,863. The revival is to some extent an artificial stimulus, due to members of the Officers' Training Corps being now required to matriculate after the fashion of ordinary students of the university.*

*Rather less than one-half of the students now attending are women, up to the end of April last there were 745 women on the roll. One of the most impressive features of the war period has been the large increase in the number of women students in medicine. In pre-war days 70-80 were the normal numbers, up to the end of April last year there were 319 women medical students, the total number of students in the faculty, men and women, being 1,056, compared with a pre-war figure of 1,500. The apparently small decline which the war has involved here is due to the fact that many of the male students have been released from various branches of the services, in view of the threatened shortage of doctors, they have received a number of valuable war privileges or concessions as regards their training, and the increase in the number of women has also helped to make good the loss of war.*

*On the personal side, the war has involved the University in serious and abiding loss. Sons of a number of the professors have fallen in action. Many of the most brilliant students of recent years have gone down. The University's total loss is difficult to estimate, but it has been put at 410. These facts illustrate the catholicity of sacrifice in the present war.*

On Wednesday, 12 June, John Campbell, a butcher of 28 High Street, pleaded guilty to supplying to a customer on three occasions quantities of meat in excess of nine coupons per week, which was the allowance prescribed for the customer's household. The total amount of meat supplied was equal

**At a Red Cross function in Edinburgh during July, soldiers played five-a-side while wearing gas masks. The novelty attracted spectators but the reason for wearing them wasn't clear.**

to sixty-three coupons worth instead of twenty-seven. Sheriff Macleod imposing a fine of £3 said he wanted the public to understand that there must be sacrifice made in regard to the consumption of meat. If such cases continued and the public neglected the orders of the local Food Control Committee exemplary punishment would follow.

On Monday 8 July, Belgian royalty visited the city:

*The King and Queen of the Belgians, who are in this country in connection with the Royal Silver wedding celebrations, travelled overnight from London to Edinburgh, where they are making the North British Station Hotel their headquarters for the next two or three days. Commander Sir Charles Oust, R.N., one of the King's equerries is in attendance on their majesties. Today was spent on a visit to Queensferry and the Forth Bridge, the visit is of a purely private nature.*

**On 15 July, the Second Battle of the Marne began. Tens of thousands of men were killed but the counter-attack at the Marne was one of the first of a series of offensives by the Allies which would ultimately lead to the end of the war.**

A story of pickpocketing in Princes Street appeared in the *Edinburgh Evening Express* of Saturday, 20 July:

*For some time Edinburgh citizens have been victimised by a gang of expert pickpockets who have been haunting the principal thorough-fares, especially Princes Street, and more particularly the east end of that street. Some days ago, a man named Thomas Gilmour was arrested in Edinburgh on a charge of being in possession of a considerable sum of money of which he could not give a satisfactory account. Another man passed the bar of Edinburgh City police court to-day on a similar charge after having been arrested by Detective-Lieutenant Mackinnon at the East end of Princes Street yesterday.*

*Lieut. Mackinnon was taking a quiet stroll along the street when his attention was suddenly arrested by a young man loitering at the east end. The man bore a resemblance to a photograph which had been passed on to Lieut. Mackinnon, and the officer at once went forward and questioned the man regarding his identity. The young fellow hesitated, and then replied that he was a munition worker from Glasgow. He said he was here on holiday and that he*

**General McCracken talking to members of the famous Zouaves' Band who arrived in Edinburgh on 22 July. The band gave two performances, one in Princes Street Gardens in the afternoon and the other in the Usher Hall in the evening. They left for Glasgow the following day.**

*was staying at a house in Nicholson Street, but the address proved to be fictitious. The man offered to take Lieut. Mackinnon to the house to prove that he was a munitions worker, the officer agreed, but once he had proceeded a few yards the man bolted onto a passing car. Lieut. Mackinnon made a dash after him, and catching him by the shoulder said, 'We will go together wherever we are going.'*

*Keeping a tight grip on him, Mackinnon marched him off, through a crowd of wondering spectators who had witnessed the*

**General McCracken inspecting the Zouaves' Band in Edinburgh during July.**

*somewhat exciting chase, to Waverley Market Police Station. After being questioned he was conveyed to the Central Police Station, where the officers found in his possession between £50 and £60 in notes and silver coins. The man at first gave the name of Wilson, but this afterwards was found not to be his proper name.*

On Thursday, 25 July, a residential club for naval and military officers was opened at 5 Grosvenor Crescent. The premises, formerly a large dwelling house, had been rented by the YMCA and furnished by them. It included sleeping and dining accommodation for thirty-five officers and areas for smoking and writing were provided. There were also several bathrooms.

The club was intended for use of officers, including those from overseas forces, who were visiting the city or passing through. The whole project was entirely funded by the YMCA.

On Friday 2 August, the *Edinburgh Evening News* reported on Edinburgh's wartime popularity:

*There was paid to Edinburgh a few days ago one of the biggest compliments ever paid to the Scottish capital. Everybody knows that there exists an "Ireland" in Canada. Well, that "Ireland", the Canada of the French-Canadian, has been put under conscription, and thousands of French-Canadians have crossed the ocean to fight a cause which well might be their own, but is not. Many of them are in England, preparing for their share in the great adventure. To a body of them fell what might be regarded as an equivalent to embarkation leave. It was put to them that they would be sent to any centre in this country that they care to visit, and to the proportion of 70 per cent, they asked to be sent to Edinburgh. There were men among them bearing such distinctively Scottish names as Campbell and Macgregor, descendants of Scotsmen who had been merged in the French-Canadian mass. There were others who had had Scottish neighbours, and there were others, many others who simply obeyed what is almost instinct among overseas soldiers, that is to "See Edinburgh". Two parties of the French-Canadians, numbering between 800 and 900, came to the city, were, somehow or other, housed and fed, and left delighted with their visit.*

*So far so good. The visit, made at little more than a moment's notice imposed a tremendous strain on the organisations existing in the city, but they were equal to the strain, and, for the time being, all's well that ends well. But what constituted a passing problem in July is expected to be repeated in some fashion or other, not once in a while, but again and again, in the course of the coming autumn and winter, and it will be the duty of the Lord Provost and the members of the Corporation to tackle a serious problem in real earnest whenever the holiday season is past and the municipal people settle down to business again. The fact of the matter is that Edinburgh has acquired a popularity that is immensely flattering, but may prove to be very embarrassing unless there is a co-ordination of agencies under the direct auspices of the Corporation, together with an adequate extension of the provision of shelter and comforts to our visitors.*

During August, the Lord Provost of Edinburgh sent a telegram to the Chancellor of the Exchequer regarding war bonds. It read:

*Warm congratulations from the City of Edinburgh on great achievement in connection with War Bond subscriptions and you may rely upon continued and unfailing support in full measure from the Scottish Capital.*

A letter appeared in the *Edinburgh Evening News* of Tuesday, 13 August under the caption 'Flag Day For Boots':

> *I vote for a flag day for "boots for the bairns", and so relieve the mothers a bit, till the government come to their help. Some of their men did not wait till the government made them go, we should remember that, and help the bairns all we can in these days of trial. If they get boots now, it may save them many an illness in the winter. I am sure no one would grudge a 3d on the bairns Flag Day, and plenty would give more. Edinburgh should try it.*

The total number of deaths in Edinburgh in the week leading up to 17 August amounted to 45. Two of the deaths were due to influenza. Of the 89 births, 42 were males and 47 were females. Fourteen were registered illegitimate.

A young mother wrote to the *Edinburgh Evening News* on Saturday, 14 September and her letter appeared under the headline 'Those Children Again!' It read:

> *Can anyone explain to me how it is while the nation's cry is to keep up the birth-rate, so little encouragement is given and almost everywhere a mother goes with her children, she is reminded of the fact that they are such a nuisance to other people? The latest snub in this direction I received yesterday and I hope the practice in not a general one. I had occasion to do some shopping in Princes Street and went into a large firm of outfitters but was politely told that I must not take my pram into the shop as that was the rule. Now it is hardly to be expected that I should go and leave an infant asleep and unattended at the door of a shop in Princes Street. What do these people expect us to do with the children? We are told to do without maids just now and release labour for munitions etc. and yet if a woman takes out her children herself she is refused admittance for her pram to the shops. There was no excuse such as want of room, as the shop in question is large enough to accommodate all the prams in Edinburgh. Needless to add, I did my shopping elsewhere where prams and infants are not debarred.*

During September, the YMCA Employment Bureau for ex-soldiers, situated at 130 George Street, Edinburgh, announced that they had interviewed 800 men, all of who were out of work. Mr Singer, who was in charge of the bureau, stated that the situation was most unsatisfactory. He said that the problem was the same all over the country and 'silver badge' men were left idle and their numbers were growing.

Mr Singer pointed out that it was difficult to place disabled men and stated that many others were unskilled.

The *Edinburgh Express* noted:

*It is quite impossible today, at the Bureau or elsewhere, to obtain skilled men. The demand cannot be met. Apart from skill, queer jobs are also on offer – such as the task of a gravedigger or a trainer of elephants. Evidently, there is great faith in the YMCA to undertake almost any contract.'*

On Tuesday, 17 September, the *Edinburgh Evening News* reported on a torpedoed liner under the headline 'Edinburgh Lady Missing':

*Two of the missing passengers on the* Galway Castle, *which was sunk by a German submarine, are Mrs Matthews (wife of Mr O.P. Matthews of the Standard Bank, Nakuru, British East Africa) and her daughter, a two-year-old child. Mrs Matthews had been on a visit to her parents, Mr and Mrs W. Williamson, 21 Eyre Crescent, Edinburgh, and was returning to Africa to rejoin her husband. No definite news of mother or child has yet been received.*

At the beginning of October, Lieutenant Righyni, an officer of the French army, toured Scotland addressing meetings under the auspices of the Scottish War Aims Committee. The lieutenant had the unique distinction of having been attached to the British, American and Portuguese armies.

He was an Alsatian by birth and stated that he 'thoroughly understood the Boche and his evil ways.' He went on to say that he had a most wonderful story to tell of all that the war meant to civilisation and democracy. Lieutenant Righyni's work was aided by means of study and travel all over the Continent, where he had had an opportunity of studying German, Austrian, and Turkish methods and had seen how nationalities all over Europe had been oppressed and tyrannised by their enemies.

Lieutenant Righyni, who, it was said, spoke English as well as a native lectured in the Oddfellows' Hall on 1 October, and on the following night in the Central Hall. There were no tickets for admission and the public was made very welcome at the talks.

A story appeared in the *Edinburgh Evening News* of Wednesday, 30 October under the headline 'Fighting The Flu'. It announced the closure of schools. The article read:

*The Public Health Committee of Edinburgh Town Council met this afternoon to consider requisition by the Medical Officer of Health, Dr Maxwell Williamson, to make arrangement for a sufficient interval being provided in the cases of houses of entertainment with continuous performances and that children under the age of 15 should be excluded from such places. The Committee decided to recommend to the magistrates, in terms of the representation, and decided on their own authority to instruct the Medical Officer of Health to give instructions that all public schools be closed forthwith. Following upon the recommendation of the Public Health Committee the magistrates met.*

*There were also present representatives of the licensed theatres, music halls and picture houses in the city who, after hearing the views of the magistrates, expressed their willingness to associate themselves with the authorities doing everything possible to minimise the danger of infection. The magistrate decided that the following arrangements should be given effect to in the meantime:*

*Picture houses having a continuous performance from early afternoon should have two sessions, namely, 2 to 5 and 7 to 10.30 allowing an interval of two hours between 5 and 7 for ventilation. With regards to places having double houses, it was decided that there should be a clear interval of half an hour between the first and second house, during which the place should be absolutely clear of occupants. It was also decided that children under 15 years of age should be excluded from all entertainments.*

*With regard to the school closing, the Public Health Committee, as the Local Authority, have this power within themselves and their decision is that they be closed for three weeks. An effort is to be made to get the order in force today.*

**The flu epidemic of 1918 would spread worldwide and kill more people than the Great War itself.**

On Saturday, 2 November, an article appeared in the *Edinburgh Evening Express* about the help being given to ex-soldiers:

*The probability of the early suspension of hostilities is necessarily raising the problem of demobilisation of men on service. The opinion of those in close touch with the operation is that the discharge of the civilian element from the numerous munition factories in the city presents even greater difficulties than the placing of ex-soldiers and ex-sailors in work. What is to be done*

**A bereaved mother and her sons carrying victory flags in Edinburgh on the day that armistice was announced.**

*with the hundreds of thousands of women in state employment? Will they go back to their old employment, with wages which were often one-half or one-third of their present earnings, and with more binding conditions? No doubt there are government plans in reserve but it is well to note that as war was waged on an unprecedented scale, there is much to be done after the war totally without precedent.*

*Meanwhile, at the principal employment exchange at Tollcross, the officials are already making headway with their task. Of 1,000 men recently discharged from the army, roughly one half went back to former employment; the other half were not in that happy position.*

On Friday, 8 November, a nurse named Mary Stewart, appeared in uniform before the Edinburgh Sheriff Court charged with obtaining goods from a number of warehouses in Princes Street without intending to pay for them. The defendant pleaded guilty to all twelve charges. The goods had been ordered for a castle in Inverness but were intercepted on their way. The property obtained amounted to £140. The nurse was sentenced to four months imprisonment.

**On 9 November, Kaiser Wilhelm II abdicated and fled Germany.**

When the Armistice was agreed between the Allies and the Germans, the fighting in Europe came to an end. It went into effect at 11am on 11 November. When the news reached Britain, people throughout the land

**Scotland rejoices over the victorious end to the war. In the photo, New Zealanders, British soldiers, women and children are cheerful as they read the news that the war is over.**

**Smiling soldiers and airmen celebrating in Edinburgh after the announcement of the cessation of war on 11 November.**

took to the streets to celebrate.

The *Aberdeen Journal* of Tuesday, 12 November carried a report under the headline 'Thankfulness In Edinburgh':

*The news of the armistice reached Edinburgh early yesterday and was received, as the Lord Provost said, with sober joy and profound thankfulness. By noon, the streets were quite a holiday appearance and the whole city was beflagged while the bells of St Giles rang out a joyful peal. The Lord Provost telegraphed congratulations to the King, the Premier, Sir David Beatty and Sir Douglas Haig and issued an order that the citizens should light up their windows at night. A demonstration was also held in the Waverley Market which was well attended.*

The war had been a long and bloody one. Edinburgh had played a major

**Soldiers and civilians in Edinburgh reading the news of the signing of the Armistice.**

part in the struggle. With the war over, there wasn't a family in Edinburgh who hadn't lost a son, father, nephew, uncle or brother. There were tremendous celebrations in the streets as the end of the war was announced but the effects of the conflict lasted for years to come.

# Acknowledgements and Sources

Thanks to the helpful and friendly team at Pen and Sword including Roni Wilkinson, Matt Jones, Jon Wilkinson, Irene Moore, Diane Parkin, Katie Eaton, Laura Lawton, Jodie Butterwood and Kate Bamforth.

Thanks also to Tina Cole and Tilly Barker.

**Newspapers:**
*The Aberdeen Evening Express*
*The Daily Record*
*The Dundee Courier*
*The Edinburgh Evening News*
*The Evening Herald*
*The Lincolnshire Echo*
*The Manchester Evening News*
*The Yellowstone News*
*The Aberdeen Journal*
*The Bury Free Press*
*The Chicago Herald*
*The Dundee Evening Telegraph*
*The Edinburgh Evening Herald*
*The Southern Reporter*
*The Sunday Mirror*
*The Western Daily Press*

# Index